Money Management Made Smart

Georgiana Golden

Published by Georgiana Golden, 2023.

While every precaution has been taken in the preparation of this book, the publisher assumes no responsibility for errors or omissions, or for damages resulting from the use of the information contained herein.

MONEY MANAGEMENT MADE SMART

First edition. October 1, 2023.

Copyright © 2023 Georgiana Golden.

ISBN: 979-8223494539

Written by Georgiana Golden.

Money Management Made Smart

Never Worry About Your Finances Again

Georgiana Golden

© Copyright 2023 - All rights reserved.

Table of Contents

Chapter 4: Long-Term Investing

Chapter 5: Debt Management

Chapter 6: Minimizing Tax Liability

Chapter 7: Insurance and Risk Management

Chapter 8: Maximizing Your Employee Benefits

Chapter 9: Retirement Planning

Introduction

Money is a terrible master but an excellent servant. –P.T. Barnum
Nothing can be accomplished without the use of money; money is life. You need resources, such as a steady income, in order to afford regular meals and housing. To keep money flowing continuously into your account at the same rate as it leaves, you must strike a balance between making money and spending it. Personal financial management is the process of ensuring that cash flows in and out in balance.

Unfortunately, personal financial management is seldom taught in schools; as a result, most people utilize money without fully comprehending it. The only thing people know is to work for a living and then spend their paycheck as soon as it reaches their bank accounts. It is challenging to handle money effectively since the vast majority of individuals are clueless on how to do it. Saving, investing, and retirement planning are the only financial management topics that are widely publicized and available. While each of these elements is essential to managing one's own finances, the *how* is lacking. What investment alternatives are best for you? How can you start saving despite your present situation? What sort of retirement plan is ideal for you?

Everyone has a unique existence, diverse needs, and a wide range of financial circumstances. The fact is that the typical working-class person does not have the highest earnings, and life can be difficult. However, it is crucial to have emergency savings, an investment strategy, a retirement plan, and general savings. You must also maintain a good standard of living, which calls for having a decent home, a reliable car for transportation, the ability to eat well, and the ability to enjoy some of life's pleasures.

All of these things are challenging, yet they can all be accomplished. And this book will cover every aspect of personal finance to give you a general idea of what you should do to prosper.

Everything you need to know about money, you will find here—but first you must understand what personal financial management is.

Personal finance is a broad concept that encompasses a wide range of subjects such as managing finances, investing wisely, saving, preparing taxes, planning for retirement planning, and much more. Budgetary control, mortgages, insurance, and other banking activities are also included. Essentially, personal finance refers to goods and services that enable you to make educated financial decisions in order to achieve your personal objectives.

To carry out good financial planning, you must first establish your financial goals. You must set both short-term and long-term financial goals in order to accomplish that. For example, you may need money in the short term to make a significant purchase or arrange a wedding. Additionally, you should make plans for long-term objectives like home ownership and retirement savings. To establish financial management strategies, you must first understand your goals, as well as your income, costs, and limits. Once you've considered these aspects, you can formulate a game plan to help organize your personal finances.

Why Does Personal Finance and Financial Management Matter So Much?

Financial planning may teach you how to manage your money, which can be useful if you want to become economically secure. Because everyone utilizes money, regardless of whether you're rich, poor, or middle-class, financial literacy is critical to ensuring your survival and security. In essence, it is a set of abilities that can aid you in distinguishing between good and bad investment planning and making smarter decisions. However, because money management is not covered in most school or college curricula, you can only learn the essentials through online courses and books.

This is where this book comes in to assist and educate readers on healthy financial habits such as understanding money and its usage, investing, budgeting, saving, creating emergency reserves, avoiding financial pitfalls, and creating a retirement plan, among other things. This is a self-help guide that you can use right now to improve your financial situation. Anyone from any socioeconomic background can benefit from this book; by the end, you will be more financially savvy and in better control of your finances.

Many people desire financial independence but lack the information to achieve it. Some people believe that working more jobs will allow them to save more money. Even the highest-paid employees may be indebted with zero savings and no real financial plan. The primary cause of this is their inability to handle their finances. With this guide, you'll gain a better understanding of how and where you're spending your money. This can assist you in staying within your budget and possibly increasing your savings. You'll also learn to handle your money and reach your financial objectives with strong personal finance management. You'll be more financially knowledgeable and have more than one source of income as a result of this. Taking the initiative to better manage your money can certainly pay off.

Where To From Here?

This guide will focus on breaking down the most significant aspects of personal finance and exploring each one in greater depth so that you have a thorough grasp of money and how to use it. Developing an effective plan and sticking to it is the key to financial management. Here, we will assist you in developing a good game plan for where to invest, how to budget, which financial products to purchase, and how to save for emergencies and retirement regardless of your income. Setting financial goals, understanding and managing credit, making long-term investments, managing debt, maximizing employee benefits, managing insurance and investment risks, minimizing tax, and using digital financial tools are all covered in this book.

A reminder that if you cannot control your finances, money will control you. Take the steps to become better equipped to handle money and let it serve you. Knowing how to handle your finances will offer you peace of mind; not knowing how will only cause you stress. So, what is it going to be?

Chapter 1: Setting Financial Goals

The best thing you can do to ensure your future financial stability and independence is to set financial goals. You can spend a lot of time thinking about your financial situation, but without clear objectives, it could be difficult to make any changes. You must be aware of where you are now and where you want to go in the future to establish plans. Setting financial goals is thus analogous to planning a vacation or business trip. You must be aware of your beginning and finishing points, the amount of time you have to "travel" (or accomplish your objectives), and the approximate financial outlay (Fontinelle, 2022).

Why Set Financial Goals?

A good financial goal will not just make your life better: It will make your finances better as well. That might seem counterintuitive at first—if your goals involve *spending* money, how can these very same goals assist you in *saving* money?

The answer is simple: by giving you something to work towards. Goals not only provide a reward at the end of the proverbial rainbow, but they also give you the motivation to manage your finances wisely in the interim. Your objectives should be significant to you—you should *want* to continue pursuing them. In short, setting them will encourage you to be disciplined in your approach to your finances. You will hopefully be inspired to change your spending habits to achieve your goal.

Having a goal encourages you to take charge of your situation in a positive way. When you incentivize yourself with something you truly value—be it your first home, a new car, higher education, or a family trip to Switzerland—it becomes easier to prioritize your spending decisions and curb excess expenses. Even budgeting can seem exciting when you've got a reason to do it. It is easier to make sacrifices or stick to a budget when you remember why you're doing this, and what's in it for you.

Moreover, setting financial goals encourages personal responsibility. It will give you a sense of clarity and purpose from the get-go, and the feeling of accomplishment when you achieve your goals will be incomparable.

By reading this book, you are already on the path to success, happiness, and security; by choosing to set financial goals, you can measure your progress along that path.

Types of Financial Goals

The next step in your journey is to assemble a written list of your goals. Putting your objectives in writing and holding yourself responsible for your success keeps you honest about how you are doing. It's also good for morale to keep track of your progress. But, before you can make a list of everything you want to achieve, you must first categorize these things based on how long it will take you to achieve each of them. Sorting your goals by time frame can help you identify your priorities.

Financial objectives can be divided into three broad categories: short-term, mid-term, and long-term.

Short-Term, Mid-Term, and Long-Term Goals

- **Short-term financial goals** can be achieved in a year or less. Short-term goals are quick to accomplish, limited in scope, and easier to plan for and anticipate. However, this does not necessarily mean they are less important. Saving for a vacation or spending less on groceries are examples of short-term goals—but so are paying off credit card debt, establishing an emergency fund, and creating a budget. The latter three are crucial components of financial success, and will all be addressed in more depth later in the book.

- **Mid- or medium-term financial goals** exist in between the short term and long term. Although they are often less critical in nature, medium-term goals are an effective performance indicator: They can help you to evaluate whether you're succeeding in your short- and long-term goals. They also serve to bridge the gap between the two. To fulfill your medium-term goals, you might need to accomplish many short-term objectives. Likewise, long-term goals are made up of short- and/or medium-term goals. Examples of mid-term goals include purchasing life insurance and getting major home renovations (Fontinelle, 2022).

- **Long-term financial goals** exist on a larger timescale—often a decade or more—and will take more than a year to achieve. One of the most vital examples of a long-term goal is saving for retirement, which will be addressed in detail in Chapter 9.

- **Big-picture financial goals** are those that will likely necessitate significant adjustments to lifestyle or income; they often take several years to achieve, and as such will broadly overlap with long-term goals. Examples include buying a house or paying off a mortgage, saving for early retirement, or attending graduate school.

Habits-Based and Numbers-Based Goals

Amanda L. Grossman—a Certified Financial Education Instructor and the founder of Frugal Confessions, LLC—posits that there are two additional ways to classify your goals beyond the time it'll take to achieve them (Grossman, 2021):

- **Habits and behaviors-based financial goals** are generally more abstract, such as "I want to pay for my child's education."

- **Numbers and digits-based financial goals** have a specific figure attached, such as "I want to set aside $500 this month."

The two can be combined with each other, and classified by duration. "I want to set aside $500 this month so that I can pay for my child's martial arts classes" is an example of a short-term goal that is based on both numbers and behaviors. It is important to ensure that all your goals take *both* of these criteria into account—if your goals don't consider numbers *and* behaviors, you'll likely end up with a nebulous goal.

How to Set and Achieve Financial Goals

A lot of us struggle with goal-setting because we tend to view our objectives in broad, vague terms. How many times have you heard "goal" statements like "I want to travel" or "I want to save up for a new car"? Having a goal like this is a good start, but how do we turn it into a *financial* goal?

First we need to examine what makes the above goals ineffective. At first glance, they might not seem to have any glaring issues, but they aren't fully developed. They're generic. They're not actionable—and, most importantly, they're not SMART.

SMART Goal-Setting

"SMART" is an acronym that stands for Specific, Measurable, Attainable (or Achievable), Realistic (or Relevant), and Time-bound. Some of the letters have multiple meanings; this is by design. Since its introduction in 1981, the SMART method of goal-setting has been utilized globally to help professionals achieve success, and the acronym itself has been redefined over time (Haughey, 2014).

As originally proposed, the "A" stood for "Assignable" ("Who will do this task?"), but it has since been adapted to "Attainable" or "Achievable" to make the system more broadly applicable to individuals. Similarly, the "R" in SMART can signify that a goal is either "Realistic" or "Relevant" to your life (Talerico, 2023).

No matter which word or definition you use, each of these acts as shorthand to refine the various aspects of your goal:

- **Specific:** What do you want to accomplish? Why?

- **Measurable:** How will you track and record your progress towards your goal?

- **Attainable/Achievable:** Is this something that is (or eventually will be) within your means? Can you accomplish this goal with the resources you (will) have? Are you able to accomplish it within the allotted time?

- **Realistic/Relevant:** Is this goal relevant to your lifestyle? Is it feasible now? Will it be feasible later? Essentially, is it worth saving for?

- **Time-bound:** How long will it take you to achieve this goal? Do you have a deadline? Can you meet that deadline?

An effective financial goal should answer all of these questions.

The SMART goal system can be applied in any area of your life, but it lends itself especially well to finance, since time is such a critical factor in money management. So many things in our lives have strict deadlines: bills, paychecks, mortgages, loans, retirement plans. All of these require ample time and preparation. "Time is money," as the expression goes. That is why it is especially important that your goals, particularly financial ones, have concrete timelines. The more specific you can get in your planning, the better your goals will serve you.

SMART Financial Goals in Practice

So how do we turn generic goals into feasible financial realities? Let's take our previous example goal, "I want to save up for a new car," and get more SMART with it. First we'll need to narrow down the **Specifics**. "I want an electric car" would be an improvement upon the original, but specifying the make and model—for example, "I want a 2023 Tesla Model 3 sedan"—is ideal.

Next, we'll need a metric with which we can **Measure** our progress towards this goal—in this case, money is the obvious answer. Google shows that the minimum suggested retail price of this car is $42,990, so there's your measurable figure. (Don't forget to account for any sales tax, and add this onto your purchase price!)

Now you'll need to evaluate whether this goal is **Attainable** or **Achievable**. Maybe you realize that a brand-new electric car isn't attainable given your budget; in that case, you might consider setting up a payment plan, taking out a loan, or purchasing a used car. You could shift around your expenses—for example, if you were to spend less money per month on take-out food and avoid making extraneous purchases, you could free up that money and put it towards your goal.

Next, we'll consider whether this goal is **Realistic/Relevant.** Perhaps you reevaluate your goal again at this stage and decide you'd rather go with a hybrid electric car, which will be more affordable while sharing some of the benefits of an electric vehicle. You might even opt for a different, cheaper model. Whatever the approach, as long as it gets you where you want to go, it's worthwhile.

Finally, we'll consider the **Time-bound** aspect of this goal. Do you have a deadline by which you'd like to accomplish it? Hypothetically, if you set aside [X] amount of money each pay period, would you be able to afford the car by a certain date?

Now you can apply SMART goal rhetoric to the rest of your financial goals. If you haven't already made a written "bucket list" of your objectives, take this opportunity to do so. Any size list is okay, but starting with fewer action items is undoubtedly less frightening.

Determine what is important to you. Place everything—from the urgent and necessary to the frivolous and distant—on the table for evaluation and consideration. Determine what can be done right now, what will take some time, and what has to be done as part of a long-term plan. Look over your list to ensure that your goals are both habits-based and numbers-based: you want a clear action statement, and some figures to back it up.

Once you've got your list, you can start to turn your aspirations into attainable financial targets by giving them each a deadline and a price. Run each bucket list item through the SMART formula. Then, start calculating the amount of money needed for the goals you've listed—both individually and in aggregate—and begin to work out how you're going to start saving.

If you want to "take a vacation to the Maldives," for instance, your stated financial objectives might specify when and how much it will cost. If your vacation to the Maldives would cost $5,000 and you wanted to take it in 2 years (for example), you would need to set aside $2,500 annually, or approximately $100 every other week.

Tips for Achieving Your Goals

Take small steps towards large goals. If you think about paying off a $35,000 student loan all at once, you might feel overwhelmed or hopeless. Instead of thinking of your debt as one formidable lump sum, try conceptualizing your costs in smaller chunks or installments. Start by paying off one class or one semester at a time, and work your way up from there. Putting *some* money towards your debt is better than nothing, even if it seems like a small amount at first. Chip away at your debt piece by piece, and eventually you'll be able to reach your goal.

Break down long-term goals into shorter ones. This is another area in which medium-term goals shine: You can redistribute your long-term goals into more moderate increments of time and money, and therefore make them more manageable.

Prioritize. Tackle the most critical goals first. Many short-term goals, such as credit card payments and rent, are time-sensitive. If you've taken out a loan, you don't want to get hit with added costs from interest if you can avoid it. To this end, it is a good idea to organize your goals in order of importance: Which ones are most time-critical? Which ones matter the most to you? Take care of the most pressing matters first, and you'll give yourself leeway to accomplish other financial goals at your own pace.

Perform regular goal reviews. Written financial objectives and bucket lists should both be seen as flexible tools. As your hobbies and situation change over time, so will your goals. Remember, the future's not set in stone. You can always adjust your goals to ensure that they still align with the life you want. If you find that a goal seems too large (or too small) for your current situation, there's no shame in revisiting it and changing the specifics to make it more achievable. Financial goals work for you, not the other way around.

Establish a sensible budget. When you learn how to budget, you'll be able to allocate funds and gain a firm grasp on what is coming in and what is leaving. If you are determined and disciplined, your budget will be able to release some money you've been needlessly spending—then you can set it aside and use that money to further your goals!

The Concept of Budgeting and Why It's Important

Budgets go hand-in-hand with financial goals. Both help you monitor your spending, both involve personalized plans, and both will benefit you immensely in the long run.

Once you've set your financial goal(s), you know *what* you're working towards; budgeting is the process of addressing *how*. In other words, if your financial goals are the end destination, your budget will be the vehicle which gets you there.

On some level, you're probably familiar with budgeting already. Budgeting allows you to keep track of your finances. Simply put, it is the process of creating a plan to spend and save money. *Process* is the operative word here; a budget's work is never done. Budgets can do a lot of heavy lifting, and help individuals to:

- prioritize their financial decisions.
- set clear financial boundaries.
- identify patterns in their spending habits.
- see where their money is going.
- identify unexpected expenses.
- identify areas where expenses can be reduced.
- stay on top of upcoming payments.
- ensure that debt is kept in check.
- ensure that money is being saved and invested towards financial goals.
- plan for emergencies in advance.

Through budgeting, you can be ready for whatever comes your way—especially if your budget includes the allocation of money to an emergency fund. (More on that in Chapter 3.)

By keeping track of your spending and sticking to a plan, you can increase your financial stability and make sure your life stays organized and on track. To this end, precise deadlines are necessary. Budgets will keep you on the straight-and-narrow path to your goals, with no detours.

This may sound like a rigorous undertaking, but when done correctly, budgeting will actually decrease anxiety over the future. It eliminates the fear of the unknown and reduces financial stress. Most people who have a budget feel more comfortable, confident, and in control as a result.

Think of budgeting like going to the doctor for a cancer screening: It might not be fun, but it's far better to be proactive and monitor your current state of affairs than it is to be caught unaware. It's easier to take care of problems before they happen. In the end, your hard work and diligence will produce a good outcome.

A good budget ensures that you'll still be able to achieve the things you want most, while simultaneously ensuring you've got enough cash to cover necessary expenses. You may be able to prevent debt, or navigate your way out of it, by adhering to a budget. And whenever you might be tempted to stray from your financial goals—by making an impulsive purchase, for example—your budget will be there to keep you on course, and to stop any leaks in your financial ship.

Many experts suggest planning out your budget for the upcoming 6 to 12 months (*What is budgeting and why is it important?*, n.d.).

Because your income and spending are subject to adjustment at any time, budgeting is a continuous process rather than a one-time undertaking. Like your financial goals, you should review and update your budget periodically. Investopedia recommends doing this every month, every 3 months, or whenever there are significant changes to your income. This will assist you in staying on course to meet your objectives.

The Different Types of Budgeting

Before you can create a budget in detail, you will need to choose a budgeting strategy; before you can do that, you must understand the various types of budgeting.

Value-Based Budgeting

Value-based budgeting is straightforward: You take care of your essential needs first, and then you categorize what's left based on how well it aligns with your values. This budget pairs especially well with financial goals: It encourages you to go through your non-essential expenses one by one, determine which are values-based and which are not, and prioritize what you care about most.

You'll set aside money towards your financial objectives and everyday needs—food, housing, utilities, debt repayment, and savings targets—when you first receive your paycheck. The leftover funds are then yours to spend however you like.

With this method of budgeting, The goal is to avoid running out of money rather than to keep track of every penny that leaves your account. As such, it is very user-friendly for beginners.

Reverse Budgeting or Pay-Yourself-First Budgeting

This is the opposite of value-based budgeting. Instead of taking care of your short-term expenses first, reverse budgeting is more goal-oriented. When you receive your paycheck, you allocate a percentage of savings towards your long-term financial objectives before doing anything else. Then you use what's left to pay your bills and take care of other expenses and wants in the present.

The reverse budget doesn't require any sort of tracking of expenses, which can be an attractor for some individuals. However, this can also be seen as one of this budget's major flaws. In order to successfully *pay yourself first*, you must already have a firm grasp of exactly how much money you can safely allocate towards future savings without jeopardizing your present. If you're too far off in your estimation, you risk sending your bank account into the negatives. For this reason, pay-yourself-first budgeting may be difficult for beginners. The focus on the future rather than the present also means that this budget may not be ideal for people who currently have some form of debt.

If you are responsible, diligent, and fastidious enough to make this budget work, you will likely find the emphasis on your goals and values to be rewarding (Siroto, 2023).

The Envelope Method

The envelope system is a classic method of budgeting that often uses actual envelopes and currency.

To begin, figure out your regular spending (or preferred spending) in many areas, such as rent, groceries, and entertainment. You will label an envelope for each category and place the proper amount of cash inside once you have decided on the amount that is reasonable for your expenditure in each one. You cannot spend additional money in a category after using up all the cash in one envelope unless you take money out of another envelope.

However, budgets are meant to help you maintain discipline, and shifting money around frequently might influence costs you can't afford to reduce. Take note that not every bill you have can be paid for in cash. These bills don't require their envelope, but you still need to include them when deciding how much money to set aside for other types of funds.

For someone who loves to use cash and wants to be tight with their money management, the envelope budgeting technique might be a smart choice. If you don't use cash but like the idea of this technique, you might be able to accomplish something similar using the functionality of your online banking program.

Zero-Based or Zero-Sum Budget

The envelope system and the zero-based budgeting approach both function similarly. However, with zero-based budgeting, you are not limited to utilizing cash, and you are not required to monitor your money in envelopes.

A zero-based budget's core tenet is that every dollar you earn should have a purpose. Ultimately, your monthly spending should match your monthly income. Thus, your budget "zeroes out", and there is nothing left over. Instead of discretionary spending, you invest any extra income.

However, this does not imply that you must spend each and every cent that you receive each month. In actuality, this strategy revolves around being careful with your spending. You'll probably have many different spending areas to consider and keep track of, as well as a strategy for handling any extra cash (saving it, for example). If you go over budget in one category, either cease spending there until the following month or take money out of another.

For someone who wants a thorough approach to money management and wants to know precisely where all of their money goes so they can make better decisions, a zero-based budget is an excellent choice. For someone who loves to utilize credit cards, this strategy may also be beneficial. The drawback is that it takes more effort than many other budgeting models due to its specificity.

65% of individuals don't know how much they spent last month, according to a Mint poll on personal finance management (Mint, 2020). But when you've planned every dollar down to the last single cent, you're less likely to overspend your current account.

50/30/20

Only three spending categories—necessary costs (needs), discretionary expenses (wants), and financial goals—need to be tracked using the 50/30/20 strategy. As a guideline, the plan works out such that 50% of your spending goes toward essentials like food and housing; 30% toward your lifestyle, i.e. optional spending; and 20% toward financial objectives like debt repayment, saving for the future, and investing.

Having said that, you can (and should) create your ratios based on your objectives and present situation. For instance, it can make sense to allocate more than 20% of your budget to those goals while simultaneously reducing your discretionary spending if you have a large amount of debt or a tiny emergency fund.

The 50/30/20 budgeting strategy can be a better choice for you if you want a less complicated way to manage your money. If you believe that having too many categories would be burdensome and you would rather take a direct approach, this budgeting plan may be beneficial. Conversely, some people may find the categories too broad.

How Do I Choose?

Before choosing a budgeting strategy, do your research and pause to consider it carefully. Consider which approach appeals to you the most before choosing it over the one you believe would save you the most money. It's doubtful that you'll follow a budgeting strategy if it seems like sheer drudgery to you. Pick one that you anticipate will satisfy you in some way. Ensure above all that this strategy suits your needs.

If you follow someone else's budgeting strategy exactly, you will nearly always wind up spending too little or too much in certain areas of your budget. Remember, you are not a carbon copy of someone else. Each person's life is unique, as is their set of circumstances. For best results, each budget should be unique as well.

Tips For Creating a Budget

Once you've decided what type of budget you'd like to create, you can get started. However, it is strongly recommended to read Chapter 3 and learn the importance of an emergency fund before creating your budget. That way, you can do it right the first time, and ensure that you're getting a head start on financial security.

The first step of creating a budget is to get a clear picture of your income and expenses. You are probably well aware of your sources of income, but the expenses you have might surprise you.

Don't forget to factor in withholdings and income tax.

Make sure to calculate your *net* income (also known as your after-tax or take-home pay) and use this to create your budget. Using your before-tax *gross* income will not present you with an accurate picture of your finances, and accuracy is everything here. The last thing you want is to find yourself short on funds because you based your budget on the wrong figures.

Observe and record your finances.

This is best done over the course of a month or more. As with financial goals, writing it down may help. Assemble all your bills, receipts, and bank statements. Pay close attention to:

- how often you make purchases
- the average amount you spend at one time
- whether these purchases are frivolities or necessities
- whether they further your financial goals

If you have a credit card statement, this can be a useful resource, because many issuers classify your purchases for you.

Review your expenditures.

Once you've got all of your transactions itemized in front of you, it can be easier to identify areas where you're overspending. Organize your monthly expenses into categories, such as grocery, transportation, housing, and entertainment. What overall percentage of your income does each category represent? Which categories are the largest? Does it make sense for them to be this large?

Search for places where you may make savings.

If you find, for example, that 25% of your monthly income goes to food (especially take-out), it may be in your best interest to reduce this.

According to Ilene Davis, a certified financial planner (CFP) with Financial Independence Services, it is advisable to find at least one thing in your budget that you can cut back on—then you can put that money towards the future (Fontinelle, 2022).

Determine how you will use the extra cash.

After you have figured out where this extra cash is going to come from, you have the more exciting task of figuring out where it's going to go. Do you have debt that needs paying down? Have you started building an emergency fund? How about a retirement fund? Would you like to invest this money, or put it towards your financial goals?

Whatever you decide, it is important to build it into your budget. Distribute the money that you've freed up into specific areas of your budget, rather than inconsistently and capriciously spending it. This will encourage you to stay financially responsible. You'll thank yourself later!

Keep your objectives in mind.

Don't forget that your budget isn't just here to save you money—it should also bring you closer to your financial goals. When creating your budget, don't lose sight of *why* you're doing so. This focus can help bridge the gap between your goals and reality.

Set realistic and achievable budgeting targets.

Make sure that your budget is as SMART as your financial goals. Move in smaller increments if necessary. It might be difficult to cut your spending in half overnight—it's not impossible! It just requires a lot of discipline—but if you focus on reducing discretionary expenses a bit at a time, whether that's per week, per month, or per category, you might find more success in your budgeting endeavors.

Don't forget about flexible costs.

No matter what type of budget you choose, you still need to budget for ongoing expenses, like cellphone airtime and data, internet, utilities, etc. These types of bills cannot be predicted because every month your expenditure will change, so you need to budget an estimated amount for them. If you have any money leftover, you can reallocate it elsewhere in your budget.

Tips For Sticking to Your Budget

Knowing that you need a budget is one thing; creating and adhering to one is quite another. To be successful the first time, you will need a few tips and tricks.

Review your transactions.

After you've created your budget, check your transactions at least once a week to be sure you're staying within your spending limit. This might assist you in making modifications as needed during the month to prevent overspending. Keeping a close eye on your transactions will also help you identify erroneous or unexpected charges early on, so you're not planning on working with more money than you actually have. Sometimes a bill can be charged early, or a payment can be late. In any case, it's best to be prepared.

Review the budget regularly.

Examine your budgeting strategy every 6 to 12 months to see if it's still effective for you and your financial goals. If not, you might need to make a few changes to better match your objectives with reality.

Adjust as necessary.

Always remember that you don't *have* to stick to your budget—at least not the way it currently is. Maybe you've found over time that your budget doesn't feel easy, doesn't feel smooth; maybe it isn't well-aligned with your goals and circumstances; maybe it's not accomplishing as much as you'd hoped. If you find that your budget isn't working for you, there is no shame in switching to something that does.

You can modify your existing strategy. If you began with a 50/30/20 budget, you could refactor the percentages and the funds they govern: instead of 50/30/20, you might try 40/30/30, or 45/35/20. Switching to an entirely different budgeting strategy might even be warranted. Remember, the goal is to create a financial framework that suits *you*.

Chapter 2: Understanding and Managing Credit

Some people use credit cards as an important part of their day-to-day money management because of the various options they afford. Others find that credit cards present unneeded temptation for careless spending that might lead to significant debt. The difference here depends solely on you.

Your financial choices matter greatly when it comes to credit. To improve rather than jeopardize your financial future, you must borrow prudently—and this chapter will teach you how. You will learn how to leverage credit to achieve your goals while simultaneously avoiding the pitfalls of high interest, low credit scores, and credit card debt.

What Credit Is (And Isn't)

In simple terms, credit is the ability to borrow money and/or access financing over time. The word "credit" can either refer to an individual's capacity to do this, or to the actual credit agreement extended to them by a financial institution. Credit allows you to purchase goods and services without having to pay upfront. In essence, it enables everyone to use money they originally didn't originally have.

In general, credit operates as follows: A lender, such as a bank or credit card company, authorizes a person to borrow a specific amount of money. You enter into a binding contract with this lender (also known as the creditor). They cover the entire cost of the purchase. The money can be accessible via a credit card, or you could be given a lump sum of money (*What is credit and why is it important: A beginner's guide to credit,* n.d.). You, the borrower (or debtor), promise to pay back the lender's money, often in installments. The thing is, there's usually interest attached as part of this deal—especially if you don't pay back the creditor's money on time. This hidden cost is why many people are wary of credit cards. If you're not careful, the interest can stack up and smother you.

However, if you know how to use credit wisely, you can use it to build wealth. When you appropriately use your credit cards, you can take advantage of all their benefits and stay away from any drawbacks that can interfere with your daily life.

Credit is money—future money that has been given to you by lenders. Just like the money you have in your pocket, you need to be able to know how to manage credit. Crucially, *future* money does not mean it is *free* money. Credit is not the solution to all of your financial issues; It is simply a new avenue whereby you can spread out your payments. it must still be budgeted like anything else. In fact, budgeting is *doubly* important when it comes to credit, as there is almost always some form of interest attached. It's imperative to exercise restraint, and treat credit as if it's your real money. At the end of the day, it is!

The Different Types of Credit

Credit accounts exist in a variety of shapes and sizes, including credit cards, bank loans, car loans, and federal loans. But did you know that there are three different categories into which all of them fall? Revolving credit, installment credit, and open credit are the three primary categories of credit. Lenders look for evidence of each of these in your credit report as evidence that you can appropriately manage different forms of debt. Knowing about each one will help you choose the best one for your financial objectives (Bringle, 2021).

These four types of credit will reappear in Chapter 5, where they'll be examined in regards to debt management.

1. **Revolving credit:** This is the type of credit most people likely think of first, since credit cards typify revolving credit. It allows you to borrow repeatedly, as often as needed, with the caveat that your transactions must all fall below a certain limit

(set by the lender/creditor). You have the option of paying off the balance in chunks over time—although there's generally a minimum payment value—or paying the whole sum off at once. Revolving credit often comes with high interest rates, which is the trade-off for being able to borrow at any time. How long it will take to pay off revolving credit is up to your discretion.

2. **Installment credit:** This form of credit entails a set payment plan over a certain period. An automobile loan is an example of an installment loan; You are obligated to make regular payments of a certain amount (for instance, $280 per month) until the debt is completely repaid. Mortgages, student loans, and term loans are more instances. Like revolving credit, it comes with interest. Unlike revolving credit, it is a one-time deal. You also know exactly how long it will take to pay it off.

3. **Secured credit:** As the name implies, this type of the credit is more secure for the financial institution, which essentially has a guarantee that they can get their money back. This guarantee comes in the form of collateral: something used by the borrower to *secure* the loan. For example, an auto loan is often secured using the purchased car as collateral. So can your home, in the case of a mortgage or home equity loan. A savings account can also serve as collateral. Secured credit is usually offered on an installment (rather than revolving) basis.

4. **Unsecured credit:** This is the opposite of secured credit, in that the borrower doesn't put up any sort of collateral, and the loan is thus unsecured. Personal loans, such as student loans, are unsecured, as are most lines of credit. Note that if your credit score is low, there's a chance you may not be eligible for this type of credit in the first place.

- **Co-signed credit:** This is a subtype of credit where an individual will sign for a loan or credit card on behalf of another person. The co-signer is then responsible for repaying the debt on behalf of, or in addition to, the primary borrower (Consumer Financial Protection Bureau, 2021).

Credit Scores

Financial institutions cannot just give out credit to everyone who asks: They need some form of assurance that you will honor your end of the agreement and pay back the money you've borrowed in a timely fashion.

To this point, everyone who uses credit is assigned a credit score. It is an official measure of an individual's reliability—their creditworthiness. Essentially, it's a way for an institution to gauge whether or not it's risky to loan money to you based on your past track record. You are said to have good credit if you have a solid history of borrowing and returning money. However, if your credit history gives lenders the impression that you are unable to pay back your obligations, you are considered to have bad credit.

A credit score quantifies a borrower's fiscal responsibility, and shows their ability to manage debt. The credit score formula most of us use today was created by FICO, the Fair Isaac Corporation. According to the FICO model's criteria, a credit score of 850 is regarded as ideal, and a score lower than 670 is significantly less so (Gillespie, 2022). In other words, the higher your credit score is, the better your credit is; conversely, the lower it is, the poorer it is.

Whether it is good or bad, your credit score will have a significant influence on your life. Lenders will view you as more responsible if your credit score is higher. Better credit scores are associated with lower-risk borrowers, and more institutions will compete for these people's business by providing better rates, fees, and benefits. On the other hand, people with bad credit are viewed as higher-risk customers, which results in fewer lenders competing for them and more companies getting away with charging high annual percentage rates (APRs) (*How to effectively manage & pay off credit card debt*, 2021).

The Pros of Credit

The most obvious perk of using credit is that it allows you to make purchases even when you don't have any money on hand. It enables you to make significant purchases that you otherwise wouldn't be able to afford if you were paying in cash (like a house or an office space). Additionally, credit enables people to buy necessities. Most individuals can't afford to pay for many things at once, from houses to vehicles. With credit, you may acquire necessary goods and services whenever you need them while spreading out your payments.

On a macro level, many businesses—and, indeed, global economies—revolve around credit. It ensures that economic transactions can be carried out effectively at all levels. When consumers and firms can borrow money, it affords them more opportunities for growth. Companies use credit to generate the goods they buy: A company that was unable to obtain financing would not be able to pay its employees or purchase the equipment and supplies it needs to produce items and turn a profit.

Good Credit Scores

In addition to this, a good credit score can open up bountiful opportunities. When used wisely, credit cards may generate hundreds of dollars in income for you just by being used for regular transactions. Once it has been established that you aren't a credit risk, you can enjoy reduced interest rates and simpler approval processes. People will be more willing to loan money to you. You might be eligible for additional financing offers, often with lower rates.

You can even take advantage of credit card rewards programs—using a credit card can result in incentives that using a debit card would not allow you to receive. Some provide rebates or cash back. Other rewards programs, targeted at regular travelers, offer considerable flexibility by allowing you to accrue airline miles and use them to pay for future trips. Hotel stays might be discounted, or even free. Best of all, you can easily get approved for more lines of credit, so that you may continue to multiply your credit on a larger scale. As long as you maintain a high credit score, you will have indefinite access to these benefits.

In these ways, credit can be an invaluable tool for your financial strength, freedom, and stability. It can improve your cash flow and allow you to build wealth over time. Money begets money, and good credit begets good things. Most people will save hundreds or thousands of dollars throughout their lives with a strong or exceptional credit score, and you will likely lose out on several financial possibilities if you don't know how to utilize a credit card effectively.

But all of this is only true as long as you can manage your credit properly.

The Cons of Credit

When using credit, it is crucial to learn smart borrowing tactics and money management. Careless use of credit products might have a detrimental effect on your financial situation. More specifically, it can lead to heavy debt. Needless to say, debt is bad enough in its own right... But if you cannot properly manage your credit card debt, you run the risk of having bad credit, which can be a whole lot worse.

Bad Credit Scores

All of the perks of good credit can come back to haunt you if you're not careful. While a good credit score nets you new opportunities, a bad credit score does the opposite.

Late fines are probably not your only issue if you have a history of paying your bills after they are due. Poor borrowing practices damage your credit. Someone with a bad credit score will basically be blacklisted from any sort of high-cash activity. Installment payments and insurance premiums are often higher for consumers with poorer credit scores. You will also be less likely to get approved for credit card accounts and loans.

In some situations, poor credit may also work against you when looking for employment. Before hiring you, an employer could do a credit check, especially if you're seeking a managerial position or one that requires managing money. If your credit is terrible, you will likely be passed over for this job opportunity.

It will become more difficult for you to purchase cars; landlords will be less inclined to rent to you; even something as simple as a cell phone contract might be more difficult to obtain. Financing options will be entirely unavailable to you, or you'll be charged exorbitant interest rates to make up for the risk of interacting with you. Just as credit giveth, credit taketh away.

Importantly, a lot of this also applies to people with *no* credit score. From a creditor's perspective, you don't have any history or track record, so they have no way to evaluate whether or not you're fiscally responsible. This is why it's so important to start building good credit early. It's a process that takes time and diligence.

Building and Maintaining a Good Credit Score

It can be challenging to survive without credit: You might not be able to make significant purchases like a home or a college degree and get the benefits of the potential wealth-building that results without the capacity to borrow and without a good credit history.

As we've covered, your credit score is one of the most crucial indicators of your financial health. It provides lenders with a quick snapshot of your credit usage behavior, and lets them know whether to trust you or not. Your chances of getting authorized for new loans or lines of credit will increase as your score rises. Additionally, a better credit score might provide you access to the lowest interest rates when you borrow money.

The fact of the matter is that there are easy measures you can take to raise and maintain your credit score. You may begin improving your credit score in just a few hours (even if it can take a few months to see results). You can build up your credit score over time by making purchases and consistently paying off bills. Not spending over a certain threshold also demonstrates creditworthiness to lenders.

Never use a credit card or take on debt to increase your standard of living, pay off debt, or make purchases that are not covered by your budget.

What Determines Your Credit Score (And How That Can Help You)

Here are the factors that determine your credit score, in order of importance (Gillespie, 2022).

1. Payment History: 35%

Your payment history is exactly what it sounds like: whether you can pay off the entirety of your credit card debt, and whether you can do it in a timely fashion. More than a third of your credit score is determined by this.

How to leverage this: Pay what you owe, and pay it on time; it's that simple. Your payment record is the largest category for a reason! It's the most effective measure of your fiscal responsibility. Therefore, paying off your debts on time and in full should always be your top priority when it comes to your credit score.

2. Credit Utilization Ratio: 30%

Your credit utilization ratio compares the amount of credit you're using to the maximum amount of credit available to you. This makes up a little less than a third of your credit score.

How to leverage this: Keep your credit card balances as low as you can. By only utilizing a fraction of your available credit, you can show lenders that you are extremely creditworthy.

Using your credit card (or other line of revolving credit) for smaller purchases will also raise your credit score more rapidly than larger purchases would. For example, if your limit is $500, making and paying off a $20 purchase would raise your score significantly compared to making a $300 purchase—*but*, as long as you can pay off that $300 purchase promptly, it can still be used to raise your credit score; just not as fast.

3. Credit History Duration: 15%

The age(s) of your oldest and newest currently-open lines of credit, regardless of how often you actually use them, are taken into account when calculating your credit score.

How to leverage this: This is maybe the easiest (though certainly not the quickest) way to improve your credit. If you were to open a new credit account and simply leave it alone for 5 years, your credit score would slowly but steadily increase during that time. For this reason, it's beneficial to keep old credit cards open, even if you don't use them regularly (or at all).

4. Credit Mix: 10%

Your credit mix—the amount of different types of credit you're successfully utilizing—makes up a tenth of your credit score.

How to leverage this: Even though it only accounts for 10% of the equation for determining your credit score, your credit mix is still a significant issue to pay attention to. Your credit score might increase if you have a variety of credit options available. Because it demonstrates your ability to appropriately use all the various forms of credit, lenders like to see a diversity of credit types in your background. Juggling multiple lines of credit also demonstrates your ability to manage different forms of debt. Regardless of your age or income level, you have the chance to improve your credit significantly with just two or three accounts—such as credit cards, auto loans, or school loans.

Obviously, if you aren't able to effortlessly maintain several lines of credit, it might not be worth the risk. It's better to have just one line of credit and maintain it impeccably than to open accounts impulsively and find yourself unable to manage the debt. That would lower your credit score rather than raising it. If there's any doubt in your mind, focus on the line(s) of credit you've already got. Remember that paying off your bills on time is *always* more important than opening new lines of credit. If you're not meeting deadlines and maintaining a low credit usage ratio, having a solid credit mix won't do you much good.

Just be mindful of applying for too many new lines of credit at one time, because this can negate any credit score improvements brought on by a better credit mix.

5. Recent Credit Inquiries: 10%

Your credit inquiries and applications are tracked, and each new account you open temporarily lowers your credit score. One-tenth of your credit score is affected by whether you have applied for new lines of credit recently.

How to leverage this: When you make inquiries about opening several new lines of credit in quick succession, it can lower your score.

Avoid opening too many new credit accounts at once, and your score will remain stable.

Additional Tips to Raise Your Credit Score

If you are new to the credit world, you might need to start with a secured credit card to establish your credit (or build it back up, if you've already got poor credit). With this type of card, you pay cash upfront to determine your limit. It essentially functions like a debit card. Credit-builder loans are also available, and are similarly designed to assist people in raising their score.

Proactively monitor your credit reports and deadlines.

When it comes to credit, negligence is dangerous. Instead, observe the utilization of your credit cards and other lines of credit. View your transactions online to keep an eye on your balances, confirm deposits, and see other activities. Report any potential inconsistencies right away.

You should also be keeping track of the payment deadlines. This will help you to be prepared. Put all of your bills in one location to prevent losing or forgetting them. Keep a note of the bills you owe, and if it would help you remember to pay them, set their due dates so that they fall on the same day each month. (Check with your lender to see if you may alter the due date for your payments.) Send your payment by mail or set up an online payment at least 1 week before the due date.

Try automating the process.

Many financial institutions offer services to make credit payments easier. They will often allow you to set up various notifications (including email and SMS) to remind you of impending payments, thus ensuring that you are appropriately using your credit.

You can also automate the payments themselves. Making recurring payments is easy and convenient when you use automated withdrawals from your bank account. To guarantee that you have enough money for the payment when it is drafted, be sure to arrange payments in accordance with your pay schedule.

You might also want to think about setting up account alerts to warn you of low account balances and help prevent late penalties and overdrafts.

Don't go above your credit limits.

Your available credit is the amount of credit that remains on a line of credit or credit card; it is equal to your credit limit less any outstanding debt. It requires discipline to manage your credit and utilize it carefully so that you do not spend the available credit on unneeded purchases. Ensure that you are not bumping up against your credit limits or exceeding them, as this might hurt your credit score. At the very least, your score will increase more slowly.

Pay what you owe, and pay it on time.

Always be diligent about paying off your bills so you don't get charged interest. Make sure that every month you pay at least the minimum amount due. You may lower your loan costs by paying more than the minimum—or better yet, the entire sum—each month. Avoid skipping any payments at any cost. Making on-time payments is a crucial step in raising your credit score because your payment history accounts for around 35% of your credit score. Think about setting up reminders for your payment due dates.

The Importance of Managing Credit Card Debt

Carrying any amount of credit card debt can put you under omnipresent, slow-simmering stress. The fact that it will set you back from your financial goals will soon seem like the least of your problems.

Debt can build up rapidly, with terrifying effects. Failing to make payments on time will have the effect of reducing your credit score over time. A lower credit score, of course, will only increase your interest going forward. This, in turn, will increase your debt. It becomes a vicious cycle. Worst-case scenario, you could become drawn into a debt spiral, where you are unable to make even the minimum payments on your credit card and are forced to seek debt relief options. Legal action may even be taken against you.

It's not over-dramatic to say that mismanaged debt can ruin your life—but the converse of this statement is that correctly managing credit card debt will improve your credit score, and your life as well.

(Strategies for paying off credit card debt will be addressed in Chapter 5: Debt Management.)

In conclusion, your credit history can affect more aspects of your life than you might have realized. Just remember that credit is a double-edged sword—when it is handled poorly, there are disastrous consequences, and you don't want debt to bleed you dry.

Chapter 3: Building An Emergency Fund

Beware of little expenses; a small leak will sink a great ship. –Benjamin Franklin

Driving a car without first fastening your seatbelt is dangerous. You are aware that anything may happen, even if you have never been in an accident and even if you believe yourself to be a very excellent driver. Wearing a safety belt is a cheap but priceless investment in your security, and you've heard the terrifying tales of those who foolishly believed they could live without it. An emergency fund serves as your financial safety belt!

As the name implies, an emergency fund is a stockpile of money meant to serve as a sort of safety net in the event of a financial emergency. Life is unpredictable. Anything can happen at any given time, and emergencies are often expensive in more ways than one. It is said that the only thing that is constant in life is change, yet far too many individuals embark on life's journey without fastening their seatbelts.

The Coronavirus pandemic has shown that even a tiny investment in your financial security may have significant effects on your quality of life. Your fund can help you avoid financial setbacks, and prevent a chain reaction of financial emergencies that could have otherwise resulted in poverty. Best of all, it will ensure the financial security and stability you need to pursue your financial goals.

The Importance of Having an Emergency Fund

Creating an emergency fund is comparable to saving for retirement: Someday it will happen, and you want to have enough money to cover your expenses when it does. While an emergency obviously isn't a joyous and long-awaited occasion like retirement is, having savings set aside is equally important. Note, however, that your emergency fund should be separate from your retirement fund—taking money out of your retirement fund to cover emergency expenses is just creating another emergency for yourself later on in life.

An emergency fund allows you to prepare for eventualities. Think of it like a bulletproof vest. In essence, it will let you expect the unexpected. By planning for the things that you *cannot* plan for, you lessen the chances of being devastated by an already-devastating event. If your emergency fund can cover the things you'll need it to—whether that be the sudden loss of a job, onset of illness, or damage to your home—you will be able to avoid taking on debt to pay for these costs.

Instead of taking out a new loan or overburdening your credit card, resulting in stacked-up interest and even more financial stress, you will have the money ready and waiting. You'll be able to take care of the emergency and get on with your life—that much closer to achieving your financial goals. So, instead of splurging what little money you have, put it away for that rainy day.

Emergency savings are not just used for unforeseen expenses; they may also enhance your regular financial management by providing peace of mind and encouraging fiscal responsibility. That, too, will help you later in life.

How Much Money Should Be in An Emergency Fund?

Try treating your emergency fund like a budget. Examine your living costs—housing, utilities, food, transportation, healthcare—and determine how much you would require to maintain your standard of living if you lost your work. Your emergency fund should contain at least 3 months' worth of living expenditure, according to several institutions and financial experts—ideally, up to 6 months should be covered (Fowler, 2022). In this manner, if you do lose your job, you'll have the resources to survive for a few months until you can find new employment.

But this is more of a flexible guideline than a hard-and-fast rule. You may wish to save more than recommended above if you have financial dependents, high levels of debt, or medical needs that you anticipate you will need to take care of. The same holds true if you work in a particularly volatile industry. If your level of job security is lower—in other words, if your risk of an employment-related emergency is higher—it is reasonable for your emergency fund to contain a higher amount of money.

While there is a recommended minimum amount for an emergency fund, there is also a recommended maximum amount. Experts recommend having no more than 12 months' worth of living expenses in an emergency fund. This is because your cash will likely depreciate in value during times of severe inflation. A sizable emergency fund might make you feel secure, but it will not offer the same opportunities for growth. If you don't invest extra money, you risk missing out on prospects for further financial development (Anspach, 2021). For millennials, who have a lengthy time horizon for money accumulation, this is especially true. Yet it is crucial to establish an emergency fund *before* expanding additional revenue streams through investment; although investing leads to long-term returns, the stock market itself is unpredictable, and returns can change in response to factors like a recession or a natural disaster (Fowler, 2022). If your investments fare poorly, you'll wish you'd created an emergency fund instead.

At the end of the day, how much money you should keep in your emergency fund is a question you will need to answer for yourself. The sum can (and likely will) change based on your choices and financial situation. Like a budget, an emergency fund is not one-size-fits all: It needs to be tailored to your life. Individual circumstances, income, and debt should be taken into account when creating your emergency fund, as should your financial goals.

Tips and Strategies for Building An Emergency Fund

Setting a personalized savings goal is the first step towards your emergency fund. The easiest way to do this is through budgeting. A solid budget serves as the basis for any financial strategy; building an emergency fund contribution into your financial planning is one of the smartest things you can do for yourself. It becomes a separate line item for which you allocate funds. Subtract your living expenditures from your take-home pay, and then set aside a part of the remainder for a monthly emergency fund contribution. That should help you estimate how much money you'll need for an adequate emergency fund and how long it will take to accumulate it. Once it is part of your budget, it will become second nature.

The next step is creating a plan to achieve that savings goal. Here, too, a budget will help. Additional funds that you could redirect to your emergency fund can be hidden in your present expenses. Making changes to your budget and reducing excess spending will free up that cash so you can use it to its full potential. A lot of things might end up being cut from your budget, e.g. buying coffee daily. That money should be used for your emergency fund instead, so you can address any problems that arise. You can also look for potential ways to increase your income on the side, such as selling items you don't need or want any longer, establishing a "side hustle," or getting a part-time job.

It's not always simple to stick to a monthly savings goal. Numerous financial commitments and temptations are vying for your attention and are ready to derail your strategy. Automating your savings is one of the greatest methods to get around this. This means that each month, before you have a chance to spend it, the money is automatically deposited into your emergency fund. You can schedule transfers into your emergency account with your bank. This makes saving easier and keeps you accountable.

Chapter 10 will give you advice on using a budgeting app or financial planner to assist in building an emergency fund.

Where Am I Supposed to Get the Money?

It is, admittedly, harder to save money when you're living paycheck-to-paycheck—but that certainly doesn't mean it's impossible.

Think back to the previous chapter, on budgeting and setting financial goals. As mentioned, it can be incredibly helpful to break down daunting amounts of money into smaller increments when setting financial goals and paying off debt. The same thing applies here.

For instance, if you need to save $6,000 to accumulate 3 months' worth of emergency savings, you may divide the amount into installments of $500 spaced out over the course of a year. Once the target amount is attained, additional savings can be set aside for other financial objectives, such as stock market investing or reducing the interest on a home loan.

If money is tight, set aside just a small percent of your income; even 1–2% at a time is better than nothing (Kurt, 2022). In the same vein, you might begin with a small emergency fund—e.g. $1000—and increase the savings over time as you're able.

In the event that you have debt, you'll need to weigh your options carefully. While it's necessary to save money for emergencies, being in debt costs you money every day. The interest you pay on one account may offset any savings you make in the other. Instead, you might choose to start with a relatively modest emergency fund target, as discussed above, and apply whatever extra funds you have to your debt until it is paid off (Chapter 5 is dedicated to debt repayment). In the meanwhile, a tiny cushion is preferable to none at all.

Different Options for Emergency Fund Savings

Finding the greatest house for your money is the next step after you've set your goals and updated your budget. An emergency account should always be liquid, which simply means that you can instantly withdraw and convert to cash at any time. Basically, you want to choose something that will be easily accessible in an emergency, but not *too* easily accessible—you don't want it to present temptation. Your emergency fund should therefore be separate from your other bank accounts. It's important that these funds be saved *only* for emergencies, and that you don't draw on them any time you find yourself in need of extra cash. Doing so defeats the purpose of an emergency fund. It goes without saying that you need to be disciplined.

In addition to liquidity, you'll want the best interest rate available, so that your money will multiply over time. Shop around and compare interest rates to find the account with the greatest yield.

There are a few different types of accounts that are especially well-suited for emergency funds. As you read about each, consider whether it would be a good fit for you.

Traditional Savings Account

This is the most straightforward approach, since savings accounts are literally designed for this purpose. However, traditional savings accounts don't often have high interest rates; your cash will increase so incrementally that it might not seem to increase at all.

High-Yield Savings Account

As the name implies, these accounts have a higher rate of interest, and thus a higher output, than standard savings accounts. The main downside is that it may take a few days to pull out your money in an emergency, especially if your account was set up online—you cannot withdraw at a physical branch location, and will often have to wait for a wire transfer or a check to go through (Fontinelle, 2023).

Money Market Account

These highly-liquid accounts combine some features of savings and checking accounts. Money market accounts often come with a debit card, which would make it easy to withdraw funds in an emergency. They often have high interest rates as well. However, you are usually required to maintain a minimum balance in a money market account—if you cannot replenish your account after an emergency, you may be fined for withdrawing the money.

Certificate of Deposit (CD) Account

These accounts differ from the other choices on the list because you must leave your funds in the account for a set duration in order to receive a fixed level of interest. You can keep your money in a certificate of deposit account from as little as 1 month to as long as 5 years. After that period is over, you will get your initial investment back, along with interest.

A CD typically offers a higher interest rate than other bank accounts. However, there is some risk involved when you lock away your emergency funds: What if you have a crisis before your CD is completely developed? During this period, you are still permitted to make CD withdrawals, but you will often be subject to an early withdrawal fee. Some banks impose a flat fee, while others could levy a percentage of the CD interest. Either way, paying a charge might undermine the value of selecting an account with a higher interest rate. It's kind of like betting on whether there will be any crises during that time. This means that CD accounts are less liquid than other emergency savings options.

Roth Individual Retirement Account (IRA)

Instead of maintaining a more traditional emergency fund, there is a case to be made for investing money in a Roth IRA. You must contribute after-tax funds to a Roth IRA, but once you have invested that money, it will no longer be subject to income tax. This can amount to huge savings over time. There also are no restrictions on when you can withdraw your contributions, or how much you can withdraw at a time. However, there are contribution limits. Withdrawing profits might also cause tax repercussions and early withdrawal fees if you are below a certain age (Discover, 2023).

Roth IRAs will be discussed again in Chapter 9, this time in the context of retirement.

Chapter 4: Long-Term Investing

Since the future is uncertain, you must be ready. This is the underlying philosophy behind savings accounts, emergency funds, and even retirement accounts. It is also the main idea that drives investment. You will learn everything there is to know about long-term investment in this chapter.

The crucial difference between long-term investment and the other forms of money management is the degree of ambition that comes with each. It's in the name, really: savings accounts are the *safe* option. In the world of finance, safety certainly isn't *bad*... But it's also not liable to get you very far.

Quintessentially, savings such as retirement accounts and emergency funds are meant to help *maintain* your standard of living—to keep it from decreasing over time. They help you preserve what you've already got. Investments, on the other hand, have the potential to change your future for the better—to help you expand, improve, achieve. In short, investment offers the greatest potential to grow your wealth.

Depositing all your money in one savings account and watching it multiply over 10 years won't be enough to help you achieve your financial goals if that account has a low interest rate—and most savings accounts do. In many cases, the rate of inflation could negate any interest you've generated. For example, you might have managed to save more than $30,000 over the course of 10 years, but by that time your money might only be worth $21,000—whereas, if you were to *invest* $30,000 over 10 years, you could end up with, say, $56,000. Banks are best used for short-term savings; the returns from long-term investments will be far larger.

Investments carry a higher degree of risk than savings accounts do, but higher risks come with higher returns. This chapter will also offer strategies for minimizing risk, to ensure that your investments will stay as safe as possible. While risk is inevitable, you should take every opportunity to avoid it.

Why Long-Term?

Just as investment beats out savings accounts every time, long-term investments will always be superior to short-term ones. This is because long-term investments have the potential to outperform the market due to interest compounding. Your money will have more time to appreciate and multiply, further solidifying your financial position. In short, a long-term investment is the best financial asset a person can own.

When you invest for the long term, you may take on more risk since a larger portion of your portfolio is committed to growth assets. Yet, despite the inherent risk, long-term investment helps shield you from very different types of risk: inflation and market collapses. If you can expect higher returns in the long run, you stand a greater chance of preserving the purchasing power of your money. Therefore, if you invest wisely over a longer period, the risk that inflation poses to your invested cash will be reduced.

In addition to beating inflation, long-term investing can provide passive income over time. You can have a portion of the interest on your investments made accessible on a monthly, quarterly, or annual basis, depending on how much you've invested. This can help you out even after you've retired—if all goes well, you'll have something to supplement your retirement funds with.

Long-term investment demands less time but more patience, and frequently calls for the investor to do nothing at all, which might be harder than it first appears. All you really need is the ability to exercise restraint—this is money you won't be able to use for a while, but it will be worth it in the end. It also helps you work towards long-term financial goals.

Perhaps you are experiencing financial hardship right now, but if you find a way to start investing, you could significantly improve your position in the future. So, even if it means you cannot save money in the short term, try to invest in the long run to ensure your financial security.

Different Investment Strategies

Now that you are aware of the significance of long-term investing, you must decide what type of investment plan or strategy to adopt.

How Do I Choose?

There are hundreds of options available when it comes to investing, which might make it difficult to decide which strategy is the best for you. Making a sensible decision on the sort of investment plan that will provide results over the long run is crucial. This decision will be mainly based on your circumstances and lifestyle.

As always, keep your financial goals in mind. To choose an investment strategy that works for your life, you must critically assess where you are today and where you want to be 10, 20, and 30 years from now (Traulsen, 2006). You are the only one who truly understands who you are, your financial condition, your goals, and where you want to see yourself in the future. Your investing strategy must be tailored to your needs and way of life.

There are attractive investment opportunities with both high and low risk. Whichever you choose will depend on your personality and your present financial status. Some people think that the riskier the investment is, the bigger the potential benefit. Others like to move slowly and deliberately so they can be completely aware of their financial decisions while watching their money grow steadily.

If you have a lot of liquid assets, you can afford to make significantly riskier investments, but it is essential to select a low-risk investing strategy if you don't have a lot of money to work with. Don't go bankrupt attempting to become a successful long-term investor; instead, invest in things that you can manage and afford. You will have less to lose if you invest within your means.

Stocks

Buying stocks is the most straightforward investment strategy, and therefore the most used. Buying and selling shares of the company you choose to invest in is the foundation of stock investing. When you buy or sell a stock, you are effectively increasing your ownership position in a publicly-traded company by the amount you are willing to risk.

When you invest in a company by purchasing stock, you are betting that it will either rise in market value, in which case you will benefit; or fall in value, in which case you will lose money. Equities or shares are other names for stocks.

Being well-informed about the businesses you want to invest in is essential for stock trading success. You must be able to read balance sheets; check the company's debt; look at its competitors; investigate the shareholder behavior, dividend history, and stock performance for a minimum of 10 years; consider the company's investment strategy; and assess the direction the company is heading in general. The likelihood that the stock you are buying will be profitable should be at least 75%. Therefore, it is much safer (but also much more expensive) to invest in well-known, established, large corporations.

To begin trading stocks, you would open a trading account with a reputable online brokerage. Create a budget for your stock trading, evaluate risk and reward, and above all remember that stock trading is not a get-rich-quick scheme. That's what makes it great for long-term investment: If all goes well, you can get rich, steadily, over time. You can also hire a stock brokerage or investment firm to manage your investment portfolio and execute trades on your behalf. The firm takes its cut, and you receive yours.

Bonds

An investor purchases a bond, which is a debt security; it is a loan taken out by a business or government. In layman's terms, when you purchase a bond, you are essentially lending money to a business or the government. When the business or government repays the loan with interest, you make money. Bonds come in a variety of forms, including corporate bonds issued by businesses, treasury bonds issued by government treasuries, retail bonds issued by retailers, and municipal bonds issued by local governments. Because buying bonds carries a smaller risk than buying stocks, the return on investment is substantially lower.

However, bonds are fantastic for long-term investment because of the interest they carry. When you hold a bond to maturity, you will receive a payout at the bond's face value, plus interest. On the other hand, if you try to sell the bond early, you may make less than the face value of the bond, and will not profit from the interest at all (US Securities and Exchange Commission, n.d.). This more or less encourages you to hold onto your bonds, and use them as a long-term investment vehicle.

Bonds can be purchased directly from the government or through a broker. Before you purchase a bond, research its financial history and make sure you're investing wisely. Also ensure that the bond is registered with the SEC, as publicly-offered securities are legally required to be.

Real Estate

Real estate is a visible, tangible, and palpable asset, making it a prudent investment option. When it comes to investing, real estate investments are in a class by themselves: Companies might rise and fall, but people will always need a home to call their own. In this way, it is a reliable addition to your portfolio. Purchasing and renting out a property is one way to generate money. In real estate investing, you can "flip" an undervalued house by making improvements and selling it for a profit.

Needless to say, real estate investment demands adequate resources. It may not be the best strategy for a beginner, since it is costly to get started and costly to maintain—due to the price of upkeep and utilities, it's a very expensive asset to manage. However, real estate investments are a reliable source of long-term passive income, which can be invaluable.

As always, there's risk: if you want to cash out, it might take months, and depending on the market, you might not even be able to sell at all (if the economy is in a recession, for example, and people are not looking to buy).

Another option is a real estate investment trust (REIT). These allow you to invest in real estate without actually owning any property. REITs are loans that you offer to businesses to help them develop and build properties in exchange for a portion of the sales revenue.

Mutual Funds

A mutual fund is a group of many investors that pool their resources to form a sizable fund and invest in one firm or a number of them. A fund manager will be chosen by the investors to oversee the investments the organization makes. Bonds, equities, real estate, currencies, and other assets are all options for mutual fund investors. The return will depend on whether it was a high-risk or low-risk investment, and the profit will either be divided equally among the group members or in percentages depending on who put up the biggest initial investment.

There is less individual effort required. You are not allowed to act alone: Mutual funds force you to collaborate with others. This can be seen as a benefit or a drawback.

Mutual funds generally carry lower risk since they are curated by the fund manager and highly diversified. However, this lower risk does equate to lower rewards. Also keep in mind that fund managers charge a fee to manage your money, which will cut into your returns (Phil, 2022).

Exchange-Traded Funds (ETFs)

ETFs are like mutual funds, in that they are a group of managed assets. Shares in ETFs are purchased and traded on the stock market, as opposed to mutual funds, which must be acquired through a fund provider (Phil, 2022). ETFs generate revenue by pooling returns from all of their investments. The portfolio (usually grouped by industry) is already assembled by a fund manager.

Each ETF is tied to a particular market index, and its financial performance will be tied to that index's performance. It might help to think of an ETF as a compilation of stocks, or stocks in bulk: Instead of investing in one stock, you're investing in several hundred at once. If those stocks do well, you'll profit.

Among the most popular indexes is the S&P 500, a list of the 500 largest US companies in terms of stock market share; an ETF that is based on this index would track the performance of all 500 of those stocks. You would profit from the returns.

Because they are more diversified than individual equities, ETFs are frequently suggested to beginner investors. Just remember that, like stocks, trading ETFs also comes with a commission fee (Beers, 2022).

Alternative Investments

There are other forms of investment that can be considered when building a portfolio:

Commodities are actual products you may invest in. They are grouped into four main categories: energy, metals, livestock, and agriculture (Investopedia, 2022). Commodities are predominantly exchanged through the stock market. One can either invest in companies that trade commodities or purchase futures, which are essentially contracts that schedule an asset's future sale/purchase for a specific price and date. Like stocks, you observe market patterns to determine whether to buy or sell.

Derivatives are a type of complex financial product: each derives its value from another asset, such as stocks, bonds, commodities, currencies, interest rates, or market indexes (Fernando, 2023). Based on how well these underlying assets perform, the derivative will gain or lose money. The derivatives themselves often come in the form of futures. They are usually leveraged, which means that they will have increased risk and reward compared to the underlying asset.

Private equity offers investors the opportunity to buy shares (and therefore have equity) in privately-held businesses. Private equity investors have a more hands-on role than most other investors. They take control of the business's operations, and revamp it with the goal of increasing its profits. The business will eventually be resold, which will trigger the return on investment. Since private equity requires investors to put forth huge amounts of capital over time, it is generally not accessible to beginners (Chen, 2023).

Cryptocurrency is one of the riskier investments out there, the reason being that it has no intrinsic or redeemable value—it is not acknowledged as a form of traditional payment in the same way as regular currencies are. The word *crypto* comes from Latin, meaning "secret or hidden"; indeed, cryptocurrencies pop up and disappear at the drop of a hat, and the sector is currently not regulated or standardized. It sticks out as a highly unstable market even in the world of investment (Phil, 2022).

Tips for Investing

Determine your risk tolerance.

Just how far are you willing to go? What level of risk is worth it to you? If you're not comfortable with high-risk investments, that's okay: Long-term investing is one area where playing it safe and choosing low-risk investments can actually turn out pretty well for you. Either way, be sure to know how much risk you're willing to take before making any commitments. You should not risk more than 30% of your investment. It's preferable to cut your losses and exit with some money than to lose everything if you have more than 20% in losses (Phil, 2022).

Determine your time horizon.

It is recommended to start investing as soon as you can. However, everyone's life is different. If you didn't begin investing as soon as you began working, it's not too late. No matter your age, decide how long you will invest for. A period of 10 to 30 years offers great returns, but if you aren't able to do 30, 10 will still get you far.

Set investment goals.

Truly, financial goals come in handy in every area. Once you know what you want to achieve with your investment, you will be better equipped to follow through. Align your goals with your risk tolerance and time horizon, and you'll be good to go.

Do your research.

Nothing will pay off more in terms of investment than self-education. As Benjamin Franklin once said, "An investment in knowledge pays the best interest." Before investing, you must thoroughly examine whatever it is you're investing in. Is it typically a profitable investment for people? Read up on the risks of different investments. Research individual stocks and companies. Assess the benefits and drawbacks. Only create and make investments with accredited firms.

Once you've chosen your investments, continue to monitor them for signs of risk. Keep a watchful eye on market trends. By performing your due diligence, you can minimize (or even prevent) the potential loss of capital.

Be patient.

Remember, you're in it for the long haul. It is important to think from a long-term perspective, rather than getting distracted by short-term returns. Don't try to time the market or pull out early (unless an investment is failing, that is). Trust yourself and your plan for the future.

Learn to manage risk.

Overall, investing is an excellent strategy to build money for the future. However, you must be aware of what you're doing and how much danger you're ready to face. Investment markets are prone to volatility by nature. When responding to the market, it's crucial to exercise patience, restraint, and control.

Every investment you make involves some element of risk, but through risk management you can reduce it and give your investments the best chance of success. Risk management involves identifying and prioritizing risks, then taking steps to nullify or respond to them. It will be addressed further in Chapter 7.

Be prepared.

Despite the fact that investing requires patience, you should be ready to jump ship if necessary. If you periodically review your investments, you will be able to withdraw at the first signs of a downturn without losing all of your money. Reviewing also allows you to rebalance your portfolio as needed, to ensure that it continues in line with your goals.

And, lastly:

Diversify Your Portfolio

Have you heard the phrase "don't put all your eggs in one basket" before? Similarly, you cannot have just one investment strategy. You must have a well-balanced portfolio of various assets. Regardless of whether you have chosen a low-risk investment strategy, anything can happen. You could lose an investment, or find it does not live up to your hopes and expectations. You cannot know which investment will yield the best profits; some will fail and others will succeed, and there's no way to tell which is which. The best thing to do is to spread your eggs across multiple baskets to give them a better chance of hatching.

To continue with the egg metaphor, if a couple of your eggs (or even a couple baskets' worth, corresponding to a bad market segment) turn out to be rotten, you'll still take a loss, but your overall portfolio will not be deeply affected—you'll have other baskets to fall back on. Diversification does not make you immune to loss, but it adjusts your risk/return ratio by giving you more options. Same return, but less risk; poor performance by one asset will not hit you as hard when you distribute your investments equitably.

For the best shot at success, you want to ensure that you're investing in different industries, sectors, and asset classes. ETFs and mutual funds are two good options to diversify your investment portfolio, as both already offer a pre-built portfolio of their own. If you have a healthy mix of investments, you will be that much more likely to succeed.

GEORGIANA GOLDEN

Chapter 5: Debt Management

Unfortunately, despite our best efforts, it isn't always possible to stay out of debt. Student loans, credit cards, auto loans, mortgages; all of these can be helpful ways to get what you need and want, but they can also be a slippery slope. Debt builds up over time, especially if you don't manage it right away. You might not even realize it's spiraled out of control until it's too late. Once you've been trapped in a never-ending cycle of borrowing, you could find yourself having to pay off debt with your whole income. You'd likely become stressed and discouraged as a result, or feel like you will never truly possess your own money.

If you already have debt, even a substantial amount of debt, all is not lost! This chapter focuses on educating you about debt management so that you may take charge of your situation and avoid a life where you are continuously making payments to creditors. Additionally, you will learn how to cope with any present debt, reduce it, and pay it off successfully.

The Different Types of Debt

We've touched on debt in Chapter 2, but just to reiterate: *Debt* is what happens when you utilize credit and spend more than you've got. *Credit* is the capacity to borrow money from a lender, governed by a formal agreement of when you will repay the amount borrowed. You pay interest (at a percentage of the money borrowed) to compensate the lender for taking a risk. The quicker you make repayments, the less interest you will pay.

Paying off student loans, credit card debt, auto loans, personal loans, and mortgages are long-term financial goals (and concerns) for many people. All of these things require sizable loans, and thus all of them result in sizable debt if not handled properly.

But the above are not categories of debt in and of themselves—they are only common examples of the four general categories of debt: Secured, unsecured, revolving, and installment. You should remember these from Chapter 2, as they are all types of credit.

Here, we'll be exploring the dark side of credit: its corresponding debt accumulation. For each different type of debt, there are conditions governing how the lender and borrower agree to accept and repay the loan (Capital One, 2021; Egan, 2022):

Secured Debt

An asset is always used to secure this type of debt, hence the name. If you are unable to repay the loan, you could utilize this asset as collateral (although this would mean giving it up).

Auto loans are a good demonstration of secured debt. If you take out a loan to buy a car, the car will be used as collateral if you can't make your payments or otherwise default on the loan. To recoup the expenses of non-payment, the lender has the right to take your car. Your assets are not yours if they have been purchased via a loan; thus, the lender has the power to seize them. You only completely own your possessions after paying off the whole loan balance.

Mortgages are another form of secured debt, since they allow for the seizure and sale of your property in the event of a payment default. To make payments more manageable, mortgage debt is taken out for significantly longer periods (15–30 years), at a much lower interest rate. Once more, until your loan is entirely repaid, you do not legally own your property. Mortgage debt enables people to take out loans to buy real estate, such as land, a home, a complex of apartments, a farm, an industrial zone, etc.

A **home equity loan** and a **home equity line of credit (HELOC)** also use your home (and/or its equity) as collateral. Each of these is therefore a form of secured debt.

Unsecured Debt

Unsecured debt lacks collateral in the form of a physical asset, meaning your house or car cannot be repossessed by the lender when you default. Instead, your credit score is used as a qualifying criteria for the loan. This is why unsecured debt frequently has high interest rates, ensuring that the lender will still make money even if the borrower defaults on the payments.

Despite the lack of physical collateral, the consequences for failing to pay off unsecured debt are no less severe. The lender can take you to court to get the money they are due. They can also use your credit score against you. After your failure to pay off the debt has been reported to major credit bureaus, your credit score will be lower, your interest rates will be higher, and it will be more difficult for you to get loans or financing in the future. To receive fresh credit, you will have to pay off your old debt.

Personal loans and **student loans** are two examples of unsecured debt. Most **credit cards** also fall under this category. The lender cannot take back any of the items you've purchased with those loans, but is still free to impose excessive interest rates or pursue legal action.

Revolving Debt

With this type of financing, the lender will set a credit limit on a case-by-case basis, and you can take out money up to that limit. Instead of paying in regular installments, you are free to borrow from the lender as often as you'd like—within reason. Your payments each month will fluctuate depending on how much you have borrowed from the creditor.

Revolving debt can be charged on a recurrent basis. In contrast to fixed-term loans, this is a loan that never expires until the borrower defaults or stops making payments. Whatever money is paid back is made accessible to the borrower once more.

Revolving debt can be either secured (such as a HELOC) or unsecured (such as a credit card).

Credit cards in particular are an excellent example of this kind of financing. Credit debt is never-ending, and you can incur as much as you want or need to. Just remember that the borrowed money is not truly yours: sooner or later, you'll have to pay back everything you owe, or face the consequences. If you are not careful, you might be indebted your entire life. The lender has the right to discontinue giving out credit, which may encourage the borrower to settle any unpaid obligations. And, as with any type of debt, you are subject to legal action if you default on your payment.

Installment Debt

Installment debt is essentially the opposite of revolving debt. You borrow a lump sum of money at the start of the term, and agree to repay it in installments at fixed intervals— for example, repaying $500 a month for 12, 24, or 36 months. The exact duration of repayment and price of each installment payment is decided when the loan is first arranged.

Mortgages, personal loans, student loans, and auto loans are all types of installment debt.

Paying Off Your Debt

Going into debt may be necessary if it has the potential to considerably improve your life—for example, if you needed financing to afford a car. It's natural to turn to loans since you will always need money to get by, and your income frequently isn't enough to support your necessities and goals, but it's equally imperative to know how to manage debt so that it doesn't overwhelm your finances or cause you stress. With these methods, you should be able to pay back your debts timeously without much strain.

Debt Consolidation

If you are in dire financial straits, this might just be your best option. Instead of making payments on multiple accounts, debt consolidation allows you to combine these balances into one. Crucially, this applies to the interest rates as well. By consolidating many accounts with higher interest rates into one with a lower rate, you can lower your overall payments, and thus lessen the rate at which your debt accumulates—in other words, you can increase the speed at which you're able to pay it off, without having to increase the payments you make.

Debt consolidation has many other benefits. For one, it makes it easier to maintain focus and keep track of your payments. Instead of having to juggle many different accounts, passwords, payments, and deadlines—which may be part of what got you into debt in the first place—you will only have one to concentrate on. This simplifies the process greatly. It could also help you avoid late fees and pay on time, because it's far easier to keep track of one account than ten. You may discover that you're able to pay off your debt much more quickly and effectively than before.

Debt is associated with stress and anxiety, for obvious reasons, but knowing you're doing everything you can to pay it off will improve your peace of mind significantly—especially once you start seeing results.

Your credit score affects many aspects of your life, and debt consolidation is one of them. The good news is that debt consolidation affects your credit score in return. If you're in debt, your credit score is probably not great, but debt consolidation can improve it. Since your credit utilization rate determines 30% of your credit score, having less debt and more available credit will quickly raise your score. All the better if consolidating your debt also enables you to make more timely payments, since your payment history is another 35% of your credit score (*The 5 Key Benefits of Debt Consolidation*, n.d.).

Unfortunately, the lower your credit score at the time of consolidation, the higher your consolidated interest rate will be. But although those with particularly poor credit might not benefit from better interest rates, and will likely end up with an interest rate of 15–36% on their consolidated debt, it may still be worthwhile to consolidate because of the potential to raise your credit score (Egan, 2022). Adding the fact that high interest is likely something you're already used to—since a low credit score raises the rates on all your other accounts as well—even a high consolidated interest rate is probably comparable to what you were paying before. Make sure to do the calculations before you decide to consolidate, though.

Debt consolidation can be done through a balance transfer credit card or a debt consolidation loan.

In the case of a loan, the bank or creditor can negotiate lower interest rates on your behalf, especially if you have a good credit score. You will be able to make one payment each month to that bank or creditor, who will subsequently pay all of your former creditors on your behalf. In addition to specialized debt consolidation loans, you may also use home equity loans, HELOCs, or student loan refinancing for this purpose.

For credit card consolidation, you may utilize a low balance transfer rate to get the debt off of high-interest credit cards and onto one lower-interest card. Be mindful that balance transfer costs, which are frequently between 3 and 5 percent, may frequently outweigh the savings from the reduced interest rate, and take that into account when evaluating this choice.

If you haven't dealt with the underlying issues, such as excessive spending, that contributed to your present indebtedness, you might want to reconsider debt consolidation as well. It is not acceptable to utilize a debt consolidation loan to pay off several credit cards with new balances because this might result in more serious financial problems in the future.

Credit Counseling

Like managing your budget, managing your debt calls for self-discipline. If your debt has gotten out of hand, a credit counselor may be able to help you take control again. A greater understanding of your spending patterns and what you can do to change them can be obtained via credit counseling. Up until you found yourself deeply in debt, you may have believed that you were just living life and that your spending was fine—but just because you're an adult who makes money doesn't necessarily mean that you know how to spend it wisely. Sitting down with someone can help you become self-aware.

Credit counseling is intended to assist those who are in debt to better understand and manage their finances. In a counseling session, the individual's financial status is analyzed, debt reduction options are assessed, and financial education is provided. A credit counseling agency can also work with you to develop a personalized debt management plan. If you take their advice to heart, you'll be better-equipped to settle your debts, and steer clear of them in the future.

There are some similarities between credit counseling and debt consolidation, mostly regarding the ways they can help you:

1. Like banks and creditors who offer consolidation options, credit counselors can help you negotiate for lower interest rates or alternative payment plans.
2. Credit counseling can also help improve your credit score by demonstrating an improved history of on-time payments, made with the assistance of the counselor.
3. Like debt consolidation, credit counseling can offload some of the burden of stress and anxiety that comes with severe debt.

More Tips for Paying Off Debt and Avoiding Future Debt

Use your budget.

A budget can help you nip a lot of finance issues in the bud, and debt is no different. Here, again, the importance of preventative measures cannot be overstated. It's hard to dig yourself out of a deep financial pit; it's simpler to avoid falling into that pit in the first place by managing your debt in advance. This is another area where budgeting shines.

You should consider integrating debt repayment into your budget directly—even before you have debt. This way you will not be caught unaware. If you schedule credit payments, including any interest, as part of your budget, your finances won't be disrupted by these additional costs. By setting aside the money in advance, you'll be able to minimize the amount of debt that stacks up.

Don't forget to ensure that you're SMART about your credit purchases and loan repayment agreements! Refer back to Chapter 1 if necessary, and set a time frame by which you'll make each payment. This encourages you to stick to a schedule, which is a great habit to cultivate when it comes to credit and debt.

If you've already identified areas of your budget where you're overspending, you can reallocate some of these funds towards debt repayment. If you haven't, there's no time like the present to take another look at your budget. By ensuring that it takes debt into account, you'll save yourself a lot of headache.

Prioritize.

If you have multiple lines of credit, knowing how to prioritize is key.

With the **debt avalanche method**, you make getting rid of debt as soon as possible your highest priority. You can even treat it as a financial goal. You'll identify the card with the highest rate of interest, and then focus on reducing that bill first. Once the debt has been fully settled, you'll utilize the funds you were using to make that payment to assist in clearing the next-largest obligation. Note that you will still need to continue paying off the minimum balance on any other credit cards that you might have (Bareham, 2023). In this endeavor, your budget is a useful tool.

Alternatively, you could use what is known as the **snowball approach**, where you identify the line of credit with the lowest debt balance and prioritize that one. Instead of largest to smallest, you go from smallest to largest. This strategy is notable for the intrinsic motivation it provides. It feels good to pay off your debt on one line of credit entirely, even if it is your smallest line of credit. Once that card is no longer an active source of debt, you can free up the portion of your budget that you would have used for repayment and put it towards your next-smallest card. Rinse and repeat.

To pick between the two, you need to ask yourself: *Is paying off debt as quickly as possible more essential than gradually reducing it by saving a tiny amount each month?* This decision is based on many factors, including how much disposable income you have left over after paying for your essential costs and how aggressively you want to pay down your debt (Bareham, 2023).

Maintain communication.

In the event that you fall behind on your payments, get in touch with your lenders right away. Most creditors are open to setting up alternate payment plans, especially if you let them know about your circumstances as soon as possible. Remember, they don't want you to be in debt either. If you are a skilled negotiator, some companies may even lower their interest rates.

This is doubly true if you already have a good working relationship with your lender. If you have been timely and communicative in the past, your creditor may be more likely to cut you a break. Regardless of your credit score, it shows initiative and trustworthiness if you keep your contact details up to date and notify your lender if you change addresses or have exonerating circumstances. Reviewing your statements early and getting in touch if you spot any inconsistencies can also go a long way.

Pay with cash or debit instead.

As a means of managing your overall debt, consider making cash or debit purchases, rather than credit. You may prevent overspending and impulsive purchases by paying with cash or a debit card, since both of these methods force you to work within the confines of what you actually have. This might not decrease your debt, but it will at least stop you from accruing more of it.

With cash, you can also avoid any additional costs that might be assessed when using a credit or debit card.

Be judicious.

If you have a solid grasp of the way debt works, you may make use of it to maintain a respectable quality of life without becoming a prisoner. Just remember that you don't always need to get a loan to purchase things; debt should be a last resort. You should only make purchases that are required, and only borrow money when it is truly necessary.

Accept one loan at a time, and endeavor to quickly repay it before taking another.

Compare interest rates.

If you must incur debt for a significant issue, check around for the best option first. Choose a loan repayment option with the lowest interest rate possible. Take into account all available credit options; borrowing money from a bank isn't your sole choice.

Chapter 6: Minimizing Tax Liability

When you work hard for everything you have, tax season can feel like an unfair setback.

We all must pay taxes; many of us simply accept this as an inevitable fact of life (though few of us are happy about it). But most of us are not as familiar with our tax rights as we should be. In fact, the government is counting on this. The IRS will not go out of their way to inform you that you don't have to pay as much in taxes as you have been; it's up to you to educate yourself and preserve your hard-earned money where you can.

This chapter aims to make that a little easier for you. Within, you will learn how to use tax planning to avoid and minimize taxes on your earnings, and ensure you are never overcharged again.

The Importance of Tax Planning

If you're like most people, you don't even want to think about your taxes if you can avoid it. The bad news: You cannot avoid it. The good news? With proper tax planning, you can not only save money now, but also save money in the future, and avoid a lot of tax-related stress along the way.

What is Tax Planning?

According to Julia Kagan of Investopedia, "Tax planning is the analysis of a financial situation or plan to ensure that all elements work together to allow you to pay the lowest taxes possible" (Kagan, 2023a). Tax planning, therefore, is something that's relevant to all of us. Nobody actually enjoys paying taxes; at the end of the day, we all want to hold onto as much of our income as we can. This is where tax planning comes in. Paying taxes is a must, but it does not have to be a nuisance, and it certainly doesn't have to be a pain.

Tax planning involves taking advantage of legal loopholes. Needless to say, if you don't understand tax laws, you'll get the short end of the stick. But if you know what to do and how to be strategic, you won't have to pay as much in taxes.

Both immediate and long-term advantages come from tax planning. Depending on your circumstances, it may put a significant amount of money in your pocket after tax season, which is the biggest short-term gain. From a long-term perspective, tax planning lets you free up more money to put towards your financial goals.

Planning your taxes is more straightforward than it might seem. You simply need to know how much you are required to pay. To figure this out, you must first be aware of all the options that are available.

Tax-Saving Strategies

You can utilize a variety of tax law loopholes to lower your tax liability. Billionaires do it all the time—how else do they get to keep their billions? You can do it too, and hold onto as much of your money as possible. Knowing and accurately calculating the tax deductions and credits that you are entitled to can make the difference between paying extra taxes or getting a nice refund.

Deductions

With a tax deduction, the entire amount of a qualified purchase is "deducted," or subtracted, from your taxable income. Since your obligated tax payments are calculated based on a percentage of your income, this reduces the percentage of federal tax you must pay. When you lower the amount of your income that is subject to taxes, your taxes will be lowered accordingly.

You may be able to deduct expenses that never even occurred to you:

1. Business expenses

Whether you're a salaried employee, a self-employed small business owner, or a freelancer with multiple jobs, there's a deduction for you.

Deductible business-related costs must be both ordinary and necessary. "Ordinary" means that it is common and accepted within the industry. "Necessary" means the cost is relevant to your business.

Deducting work-related expenses and other out-of-pocket costs that are typical for the sort of work being done is one way for people who run a small business to reduce their tax burden. You are able to deduct any costs incurred in the operation of your business, as long as they are within the IRS's guidelines.

Every income is subject to a Federal Insurance Contributions Act tax of 15.3%, which the government uses to fund the Medicare and Social Security programs. Employers share the expense with their employees, while self-employed people are responsible for covering the full cost. If you are self-employed, the state will let you reclaim 50% of the money paid from your revenue taxes to make up for the additional cost.

The practice of having a side hustle in the twenty-first century qualifies you for several tax benefits, so you may be able to save a lot of money on taxes through your freelancing work or time spent driving for ride-sharing services. Business-related shipping, ad campaigns, office supplies, web application fees, the percentage of wired internet charges used for work, membership fees, and business-related travel are just a few of the expenses that can be deducted.

If you use your new car to get to work, its entire value may be deductible as a business expense. If you work from home, that new laptop is deductible too. If you're a business owner or a self-employed individual, you can deduct 50% of the cost of business meals (IRS, 2022).

2. Charitable donations

Contributions to eligible charitable organizations can also lower your taxes if you itemize deductions on your tax return rather than accepting the standard deduction. Money or products, such as apparel or household goods, are also acceptable forms of contribution. But, to claim a donation that is worth more than $250 as a deduction, you must have a receipt.

3. Mortgage interest

For your first or second home, the IRS allows you to deduct mortgage interest on the first $750,000. However, there is no standard deduction for mortgage interest, so you must itemize it on your taxes.

4. Health savings account contributions

If you have a high-deductible medical plan that qualifies, making contributions to a health savings account is another approach to reducing taxable income. These accounts provide tax-deferred growth, tax deductions on contributions, and tax-free withdrawals for eligible medical costs. Comparable to investments in a retirement account, any sum that is left over at the end of the year can be carried over continuously.

Tax Credits

Rather than reducing your taxable income, tax credits directly lower the amount of taxes you need to pay. If the amount of the tax credit exceeds the amount of tax you owe, you may be eligible for a tax refund in the amount of the difference. There are specific credits you may qualify for. All of these are listed on the IRS's website. Some credits aren't calculated based on the difference between credits and taxes, and may provide a refund even if you do not owe any tax that year (IRS, 2023).

The **earned income tax credit** aims to help lower/middle-class workers to cover basic living costs. If you are a US citizen who has earned less than $59,187 in income, you will likely qualify. You can retroactively apply for this credit on your past 4 years of tax returns.

The **child tax credit** allows you to claim a credit for a child who is listed as dependent on your taxes; this child can be a relative or a foster/step child, but they must live with you at least half the time, be under 17, and be an American citizen.

The **American opportunity tax credit** is designed to help with the expense of higher education. To qualify, a student must be enrolled at least half of an academic period (semester, trimester, etc.) while pursuing a degree or similar credential. This credit can be claimed for up to 4 years, and qualifying students can receive a credit of up to $2,500 per year.

The **lifetime learning credit** is also targeted at college and university students: it will cover up to $2,000 of courses and education-related expenses per tax return.

Deferring Your Taxes

There are legal methods for postponing the taxes that you owe, rather than getting rid of them entirely. You will still be required to pay these taxes in the future, but will be absolved for the current tax year. The main advantage of deferring your taxes is that it gives your investments, assets, or retirement account contributions another year to grow tax-free. You have the potential to increase your earnings while your level of tax stays the same. You also buy yourself some time.

Tax-Loss Harvesting

As you probably know, you are taxed on the capital gains you make through successful investments. In tax-loss harvesting, you offset this capital gains tax with your capital losses. The concept is similar to a tax deduction, but applies to investments and assets instead. Many investors will incur capital losses on purpose by selling an asset at a loss, purely so that they can subtract that asset from their taxes for that year. Thus, the loss is "harvested" to the investor's benefit.

It is important to note that tax-loss harvesting does not actually negate or decrease the amount of taxes that you owe—simply defers it for another year. The point of this method is to free up money for short-term use, ideally so that you can reinvest it for higher gains (Kopp, 2022).

Tax-Advantaged Retirement Account Contributions

The money you put into IRA and 401(k)/pension funds cannot be used as a tax deduction, but all of these accounts are tax advantaged. You will not pay tax on any contributions you make to these accounts—at least not initially—which makes it easier to save.

Traditional IRA contributions are either tax-free or tax-deferred, depending on your specific account. These contributions may also be tax-deductible.

Pre-tax accounts, such as 401(k)s, allow you to make contributions before your income is taxed. These contributions are deductible for the current tax year. This lowers your overall taxable income, and therefore your tax burden. The more money you invest in your 401(k), the less you will have to pay in taxes.

Roth IRAs work the opposite way. They are established using money that has already been taxed, so that money will be immune to taxation thereafter. Earnings in a Roth account accumulate tax-free and can be accessed tax-free in retirement, even though you don't get a tax deduction.

Tax Planning Tips

Track expenses that can be used for deductions or credits.

Even the IRS notes that "It's important to determine your eligibility for tax deductions and tax credits before you file" (IRS, 2023). The keys to tax planning are thinking ahead and keeping detailed records of all your transactions. Save those business receipts—you're going to need them!

If you're pondering buying, selling, or renting a property, check the available credits and deductions. Energy-efficient home improvements, for example, may earn you a tax credit that offsets the purchase price of a new house.

Maximize your retirement contributions.

Tax-advantaged accounts like 401(k)s and IRAs have a maximum amount that you can contribute to them at one time. Unlike your credit card, you definitely want to max out your retirement accounts. By contributing the highest possible amount of your income each period, you're also reducing your tax burden by the greatest possible portion. Saving for the future at the same time is a bonus.

Plan ahead.

It's a good idea to evaluate every purchase you make. Can it be used to reduce your taxes in some way? If you base all your spending decisions around this, you can maximize your tax savings.It's important to consider the potential ramifications of your purchases as well. You should also periodically review your estimated taxes for the current year. If applicable, review your employer's tax withholdings in advance. This will give you a good idea of your tax liability and what to expect.

Review your last tax return.

Reviewing your last tax return may help you to identify missed opportunities, and spot new opportunities going forward. Errors may be present in your taxes. If you didn't report any deductions or tax credits, but you've since found out that you qualify for some, you can amend your tax return—you may be able to get a tax refund from the IRS.

The Benefits of Working With a Tax Professional

You probably know the inherent stress of filing taxes all too well. *Are these numbers really right? Why do I owe that much? Have I messed up somewhere? I don't have time for this!* It takes a lot of effort to figure out what you can and cannot deduct, fill out tax forms correctly, and sift through documents. When you complete your tax return without expert help, there is always a danger that you will make mistakes because you are doing things on your own—and mistakes might lead to fines and increased tax debt. Tax professionals can help you avoid this headache.

Just as it's beneficial to get someone else to read over an essay or manuscript before submitting it, having a fresh set of eyes on your taxes can help you immensely. For starters, it's more efficient. The sheer amount of regulations involved in tax preparation can be cumbersome at best, but tax professionals are well-versed in these complex laws and processes so that you don't have to be. They can catch any mistakes you might have been making, and ensure that you're not missing any opportunities. While the government will not tell you which tax deductions you could be taking advantage of, a tax professional certainly will.

Like your budget, your retirement plan, and everything else, your taxes are specific to your situation—no other person has the exact same finances. Tax consultants can offer advice tailored to your circumstances. There are deductions or credits for just about everything, and a tax consultant can help match them to your life.

A tax professional can serve as a guide even outside of tax season. You can (and should) run major financial decisions by your tax consultant, who will tell you how these choices may impact your taxes. This is the process of tax planning at work: looking into the future to see how each decision will impact your taxes. Seemingly-innocuous investments can have dire tax implications, but other actions can save you money in the long run. A tax professional can help you tell these apart.

The legal aspect should not be ignored. A tax professional can help prepare and file your taxes for you—you'll avoid any fees for filing late. And, in the event of an audit or a dispute with the IRS, a tax professional can even serve as court representation. The fact is, tax professionals will always be more knowledgeable about legal loopholes than you are, so sit back and let them do their work.

Chapter 7: Insurance and Risk Management

Nothing is more important than your life and your ability to make a living. So it makes good sense to insure your greatest asset: you! –Calvin Coolidge

As we established in Chapter 3, anything can happen at any time. Risk is an inherent part of life. There are situations when an emergency fund may not be sufficient to cover your losses, particularly if you have lost investments or retirement funds. The future is uncertain; a business, a bank, or an entire economy might collapse overnight, costing you every dollar you've been saving or investing. In cases like this, you need to have a backup plan.

This chapter aims to educate you on adopting the proper safety measures for your money. Making sure you have insurance and an effective risk management strategy is the fallback plan you need. Safeguarding your finances is a form of self-defense, since you will be the one who suffers if something bad happens. When it comes to money, you need to take every precaution.

The Importance of Risk Management

We briefly touched on this concept in Chapter 4. As a refresher, Investopedia defines risk management as "the process of identification, analysis, and acceptance or mitigation of uncertainty in investment decisions" (Kenton, 2021).

Think of risk management as the other half of an emergency fund. Just as budgeting is the vehicle to achieve your financial goals, risk management is the more action-oriented part of emergency planning. The emergency fund is the money; risk management is the plan. Both are preventative measures that protect against potential losses and disasters. Again, the key is to expect the unexpected—to take steps to prepare for the worst *before* it happens. In doing so, you can reduce the fear of uncertainty, and live comfortably knowing that you'll be financially stable, if not secure, when something inevitably goes wrong.

Risk management is not just a fallback plan: It also helps separate untenable risks from those risks worth taking (Tucci, 2023). Your investment decisions should be founded on risk management.

The Importance of Insurance

What an emergency fund is to your finances, insurance is to your life. It's an investment in your health and safety, and a textbook example of risk management.

Many would argue that you cannot place monetary value on a human life; the insurance industry would disagree. Insurance is a contract an individual makes with an insurance company. The individual puts up money in advance, and the company agrees to financially protect or reimburse them if a particular loss occurs. This contract is known as an insurance policy. Each one has a policy limit, which is the maximum amount of money that the insurance agent will pay out in the event of a loss.

When you start making insurance payments, you are requesting that the insurer absorb your risk. An insurance policy's price, or premium, corresponds directly to the likelihood that a risk or event may manifest. You will pay a higher premium if the risk is high, and a lower premium if the risk is low. Fortunately, higher premiums also equate to higher payouts.

It's analogous to betting money that a particular catastrophe will happen. If you're correct, the money you've "bet" will cover any expenses incurred by that event. Insurance money is your ace card: It serves as your final line of protection in case things go wrong. If the disaster you've insured against never occurs, you'll lose your money, but it could be worse—you'll still have your life.

Keep in mind that even insurance isn't completely dependable. No risk management strategy is foolproof. Insurance is only a safety measure, not a guarantee.

Different Types of Insurance

Almost everything may be insured against; an insurance policy exists for every scenario that can arise on earth. These various policies also stand for the values held in society. This list shows what motivates people and what society views as vital enough to be covered by insurance.

Health Insurance

Simply put, the point of health insurance is taking care of your medical needs. It is intended to cover costly or severe illnesses as well as those that require prolonged hospitalization. Health insurance may either cover the costs as they arise, or reimburse you for the cost of care afterwards.

That said, each insurance plan is different. Some are more comprehensive than others. Depending on your specific plan, more expensive or complex procedures (such as MRI scans) might not be covered at all, and you may still be required to pay out-of-pocket. You might also have what is known as a copay, where your insurance covers only a portion of the treatment, and you pay for the rest.

Here are some of the general costs that can be covered by health insurance (Acko, 2023):

- hospitalization

- any bills resulting from hospitalization, i.e. post-surgery care or an ambulance ride to the hospital (if medically necessary)

- most prescription medications

- the treatment of chronic and acute illnesses

- surgical procedures

Until 2019, people who did not have health insurance coverage were subject to tax penalties, and required to pay fines to the IRS. These fines equaled "up to $695 per uninsured adult or 2.5% of your income"—whichever number was higher (Crail, 2022). Although this part of the Affordable Care Act has since been repealed, some states have enacted their own provisions whereby people without health insurance must pay fines, essentially recreating it at a state level rather than a federal level. Although one could make the argument that it was harsh to penalize already-vulnerable people for being uninsured, the ACA points to the universal importance of health insurance.

Life Insurance

The fragility of human life is one of the reasons it is so valuable. It can easily be lost to diseases, accidents, or murder. When you are gone, the people that remain (family, friends, colleagues, etc.) are left with a financial gap that needs to be filled. This is why life insurance was created. Its purpose is to provide financial security for your loved ones after you pass away, at the projected worth of your life.

Whole life and term life are the two forms of life insurance available. Term life insurance allows you, the policyholder, to be able to take part of the funds at a set time so that you may also enjoy some of the money before you pass away. Whole life insurance is only accessible by your named beneficiaries once you have passed away.

Property or Homeowners Insurance

All potential damages—vandalism, fire, water and heat damage, theft, cracks, etc.—can be covered by property insurance. Property is a worthwhile investment, and for it to maintain its value, you must be sure that it is covered by insurance. Multiple forms of property insurance exist. You can get insurance coverage to prevent losing your property in the event you cannot pay anymore. If, for example, you lose your job and have a mortgage, your insurance will cover the outstanding debt. You can obtain insurance that will cover the cost of rebuilding your home or buying a new one if it sustains severe damage from a fire or other causes.

Auto Insurance

On a regular basis, expensive accidents will occur on the road—you never know when this will happen to you. Regardless of whether you caused the collision or not, you must have the money to cover your vehicle and any medical costs. If you were at fault, you will also need to pay for damage to the other party's car. These expenses are covered by auto insurance. Third-party car insurance only covers damages to the other person; comprehensive insurance protects both you and the person you crashed into.

Disability Insurance

Accidents at work or on the road can happen at any time, leaving you incapacitated and unable to do the job you used to do. If you become disabled, you likely won't be able to work, and, depending on the severity of your condition, you could be bedridden. Life might get challenging if you don't have a steady source of income, but you can get a disability insurance policy, which is intended to provide financial protection against all potential impairments that can happen in the future. Depending on the type of coverage you select, you will either get a lump sum or ongoing payments into your account.

Long-term Care Insurance

Disability insurance covers the income that will be lost in the event that you become disabled, whereas long-term care insurance covers expenses directly related to your care. In addition to disabilities, plenty of other rare and hereditary conditions can leave you in need of help. It's possible that your friends and family won't be able to help you when you need them, since being a caretaker is a full-time job. Long-term care insurance will pay someone to do that job for you, whether this is a specialized nurse or caretaker who visits your home or a long-term care facility where you will live. If it's the latter, long-term care insurance will also cover the costs of moving there. You can be assured (and insured) that your daily needs will be taken care of.

If your family history includes a history of chronic diseases, you should consider this form of insurance coverage.

Liability Insurance

Accidents can occur at any time, causing serious injury or death to the person you collided with. You could accidentally cause damage to someone else's property or become engaged in one. Because you are at fault for the harm or death, you are vulnerable to civil lawsuits and claims when such things happen. This insurance coverage can assist in covering those claims. An insurance policy that covers accidents in life is liability insurance.

Umbrella Insurance

Umbrella insurance provides additional protection above and beyond what is typically provided by home or auto insurance. It offers an extra measure of protection to individuals who run the possibility of facing legal action for injuries they inflict in accidents or property damage they cause to others. Moreover, it defends against invasions of privacy, defamation, sabotage, and litigation. Those who have substantial assets or potentially dangerous items are the people who should consider getting umbrella insurance coverage; the same is true for people who participate in activities that might raise their chances of being sued.

Travel Insurance

Possessions that are damaged or stolen while traveling, whether locally or abroad, are covered by travel insurance. This coverage is best for frequent travelers; if you only travel occasionally, it is not cost-effective to get it.

Cyber Insurance

In today's world, everybody has a digital profile and digital footprint, which could be used by cybercriminals to access your sensitive personal data. Cyber insurance is intended to address online risks; individuals with enterprises are better suited for this sort of insurance. You can obtain this kind of coverage if you are a person with significant money and assets. Otherwise, it is advisable to get protection and antivirus software instead.

Is Insurance Worth It?

To answer that question, you must weigh the risks and benefits of each type of insurance. Would it be worse to need insurance and not have it, or have insurance and not need it? The answer, at the end of the day, depends on you.

Before deciding to get insurance, you should consider what is most pertinent to your needs and way of life. You need to cover the important things, and *only* the important things. Do not over-insure yourself. If you buy more coverage than you really need, you'll end up with less money leftover to spend on other necessities. The chances you'll get into an auto accident are moderate; the chances you'll also separately get hit by lightning, fall victim to theft, get hacked, and watch your house burn down are slim. While it is essential to have some form of insurance, it is a bad idea to purchase all of them. That will only drain all of your funds. You already need to budget money for retirement, investments, and savings.

A couple of guiding questions might be:

1. Can you pay for whatever it is that you are seeking to cover?
2. What is the likelihood that the risk may materialize?

For example, if you decide to purchase smartphone insurance, what are the chances of it being damaged or stolen? Is it reasonable to pay premiums for this? A phone can easily be replaced out of pocket. Your life, on the other hand, cannot.

For your protection, you should cover any sizable assets and resources you have. For situations that won't put a significant burden on your financially, insurance is not necessary. Start with your essential requirements (house, car, and company), then go on to more complex or specific requirements (cyber, travel). If you change your mind, you may always increase coverage in the future. By purchasing the right insurance now, you may reduce your risk and increase your savings.

Tips to Choose and Manage Insurance

Shop around.

There are as many insurance providers as there are types of coverage. Don't settle for the first policy you find—do some comparison shopping to find the best coverage at the best price. There may be discounts that you can take advantage of.

Be prepared.

When signing up for a policy, make sure you know what to do and what to expect if that risk ever materializes. In the event that you need to file a claim, you should understand the process of doing so.

To make it easier for yourself, consider keeping documentation of your insurance policies and any claims you might have to file; this will save you from having to look the information up later.

Being prepared also means researching the tax implications of the insurance policy, and the federal and state regulations that govern insurance.

Consider the deductibles.

Deductibles are a key element of insurance policies, put in place to prevent people from making excessive claims for insignificant events. A deductible is a preset amount of money that you must pay out of pocket in order to receive your claim payout (Kagan, 2023c). If you are at higher risk for a particular event, you will want to opt for a lower-deductible plan in case it does. For instance, a taxi or rideshare driver has a higher chance of traffic accidents, simply because they spend more time in the car. If this driver became involved in multiple collisions, a plan with a costly deductible would not be a wise choice.

Read the fine print.

It's essential to check each insurance policy carefully, because some insurance providers may be cunning and refuse to pay claims because of a technicality or specific contract provision. Before agreeing to pay for insurance, be sure you understand the intricacies of what you are signing. Exclusions and limits make the difference between a good policy and a bad one.

Insurance is more stable than other industries during a recession. This is because people and companies may always be protected from risks, regardless of the state of the economy. It might be challenging to find a self-insurance policy that provides complete coverage at a fair price. Searches take time, and frequently you don't realize the policy isn't good for you until you've carefully read the policy's terms (Huddleston, 2023).

Time is a factor, too. Depending on the situation, you might not be able to afford the wait if your insurance company pays out claims over time.

Examine your insurance requirements once a year.

Your insurance plan will change as your needs do. Perhaps after getting car insurance for your primary vehicle, you've bought a new vehicle, or perhaps you now work from home and no longer drive.

It's crucial to think about whether your policy needs to change to accommodate life changes.

remain on top of your insurance needs, stay in touch with your insurance carrier or agent.

Avoid postponing payments.

Most insurance is charged monthly. Payment default is seen as a poor risk, which may result in a higher rate. You always need to make your payments on time without fail. With some policies, you might have difficulty claiming if you have a history of missing payments. In the event of insurance renewals, you must provide the insurer with prompt written notice if you decide not to renew your policy. Remember that if you transfer insurance companies before your policy is due for renewal, you can be charged a penalty for canceling your coverage too soon.

The Benefits of Working With an Insurance Professional

Because there are so many elements to take into account while getting insurance, you may consult insurance specialists who can assist you in finding the best insurance coverage to meet your needs.

By using an insurance broker, you can sometimes have your insurance coverage negotiated on your behalf, which will assist you to get the best insurance policy on the market. To get the best coverage, an insurance broker will do a gap and market study, to find out your needs and how to match them with the market. In addition, the broker will ensure that you understand what you're receiving out of the insurance, and provide appropriate explanations of the laws, claims, and contract inclusions and restrictions of your policy.

Chapter 8: Maximizing Your Employee Benefits

If you know how to get the most out of your employer, working a 9-to-5 job is not entirely useless. This chapter will teach you how to get the most out of the benefits your company provides you.

But even if you don't currently work for a company, stay tuned. Yes, for employee benefits—but also for tips on negotiating your salary, which will come in handy when you're looking for your next job. (Who knows? That future job might have benefits, too.)

Employee benefits are one of the most useful tools in your financial arsenal—and one of the most overlooked. A lot of people aren't even aware of what their company's benefits are, let alone how to use them. Knowledge is power, and familiarizing yourself with your benefits can get you far. But remember that knowledge is only half the battle. At the end of the day, your employee benefits still serve a supplementary role to your overall income. You shouldn't just be getting paid in perks: you should be getting paid in cash!

Just as many employees are either unaware of benefits or don't use them, negotiating for compensation is a frequently disregarded—and extremely effective—method of enhancing one's financial situation. The latter half of this chapter will teach you how to negotiate a compensation package that will make it worthwhile for you to get up in the morning and go to work every day. You might come to find out that you're eligible for some perks that you weren't even aware existed, and you'll hopefully walk away with more money in your pocket.

Understanding and Making the Most of Employee Benefits

Though some people might write these off as simply *nice-to-haves*, others may choose their job specifically for the perks and opportunities it will provide them. According to a 2015 survey conducted by Glassdoor, 57% of people—nearly three out of five—reported that employee benefits are among their top criteria when it comes to selecting a job (Glassdoor Team, 2016).

Employee perks are also advantageous for the employers who offer them. Rewarding employees through benefits is a way to build loyalty and ensure that people feel valued within the organization. By watching out for the health of employees and offering them the opportunity for growth, employers can

- improve employee morale and satisfaction
- foster relationships within the company
- motivate employees to perform at their best
- create a positive company culture
- attract and retain highly talented individuals
- minimize the risk of workplace accidents

By selecting an employer who offers competitive benefits, you can be assured that your contributions to the company will be valued.

Most importantly, employee benefits can provide significant financial and personal benefits, as well as security and stability, to employees and their families. Employee benefits can help to provide additional compensation beyond salary, and close the gap between living expenses and your financial goals. By taking advantage of your benefits, you can bring your plans for the future closer to fruition. You may even save up enough money to start reshaping your present life. So why wait? Take the time and make the effort to use your compensation plan in full.

Types of Employee Benefits

Because employers are required by law to offer benefits, you have access to many perks as an employee. The majority of individuals are aware of the typical perks provided by their companies, including paid time off, 401(k) retirement plans, and health insurance. But this is far from a comprehensive list! There are additional advantages that employees can, and should, take advantage of.

While you might not be able to use all of them, you should still be able to benefit from a handful that will give you and your family peace of mind. If exploited wisely and correctly, each of these benefits might save you thousands of dollars. Instead of covering your necessities out of pocket, why not have your employer do it for you?

Financial Benefits

Some employee perks are directly financial in nature. The worth of these can be easily measured: these types of benefits usually have a dollar amount attached. You can utilize these to expand your financial options.

Health Savings Accounts (HSAs) and Flexible Spending Accounts (FSAs)

Both of these accounts are tax-advantaged, and intended to help you cover eligible out-of-pocket medical expenses. Your employer may make contributions to these accounts on your behalf.

To qualify for an HSA, you must have a high-deductible health insurance plan (HDHP). You may reduce your total costs for items like prescription medicines, copayments, and deductibles by wisely using your HSA. There is a cap on the amount you may deposit each year, but you can carry over any undeposited balance to the following year, letting you budget for large costs. Also, all interest and other account earnings are tax-free. Similarly, FSAs are used to pay for out-of-pocket expenses, with the key difference that your balance will not carry over—you must use it or you will lose it.

Retirement Plans

Your workplace may provide 401(k)s or Roth or traditional IRAs. Retirement funds and contributions are some of the best benefits a workplace can offer its employees. As established in the last chapter, these accounts are tax-advantaged, and are critical to your long-term financial stability. They will be discussed again in the next chapter.

If you are qualified for a retirement plan with matching contributions, make sure you contribute the maximum amount of money to get the largest possible matching contribution from your employer.

Workplace Benefits

These are some of the most common and well-known benefits—as well as some of the most integral ones, as they directly impact your work life and your ability to function:

- paid time off (PTO)
- vacation time
- paid holidays
- sick leave
- maternity or parental leave
- paid childcare
- flexible workplace hours

Workplace benefits also come in the form of discounts, incentives, and perks. For example, if you work at a supermarket, you might get 20% off your groceries. If you are a restaurant employee, you may receive complimentary meals. Phone and cable companies might give you discounted memberships, premium services, or special plans (including family plans). For other roles, you could have access to company-provided vehicles, or the company might reimburse your transportation costs instead. Employers could provide access to an employee credit union, tickets to nearby athletic and cultural events, home maintenance services, special pricing on household supplies, and more.

While these types of benefits are not monetary themselves, they should not be overlooked, as they have the potential to save you a lot of cash in the long run. If your company, for example, has a legal department that is also open to employees, you may make use of this benefit to arrange your affairs, and save money by not having to pay a lawyer out of pocket to buy property, create a will or trust, etc. So, although having extra funds is good, you should consider the worth of different possibilities. By taking advantage of the reductions your company has negotiated, you might perhaps save hundreds or thousands of dollars a year.

Healthcare, Life, and Wellness Benefits

Insurance

Health insurance, dental insurance, vision insurance, life insurance, disability insurance, long-term care insurance, and more may be covered by your employee benefits.

Your workplace may also provide programs and incentives, which promote healthy lifestyle choices and can help to reduce healthcare costs.

Employee Assistance Programs (EAPs)

An EAP is a service made available by third parties to help employees who are having problems in their personal life away from work. Treatment for substance addiction, legal aid, spousal or individual therapy, adoption support, and other services may be included. Nobody at your workplace will know what services you've utilized because everything is private. You'll gain access to reputable service providers that have been thoroughly verified at a discounted rate.

Similarly, if you have issues in your professional life, you may be able to receive career counseling or mentorship.

Educational Support

An increasing number of companies are including student loan benefits in their employee benefits package as a result of the skyrocketing student debt.

If you still have loans to pay off, you might want to research this benefit as it is not very prevalent but is growing. Several businesses also provide tuition reimbursement or career development financial aid to pay for the costs of training, workshops, materials, and credentials for workers who want to improve their education. Using employee perks that can advance your knowledge, increase your marketability, and perhaps increase your pay is a wise decision for both your career and your wallet.

Tips and Strategies to Maximize Employee Benefits

Research the available options.

Though it may sound obvious, the first step towards maximizing your benefits is knowing what they are. You should familiarize yourself with all of the employee benefits offered by your company. While some might be included from the get-go, you'll likely have to opt in to receive others.

To learn about the perks you may be missing out on, check your employee portal or speak with a human resources advisor, who can assist you in learning about your eligibility and the registration process. Examine your whole employment benefits package to make sure you are aware of all the ways it may improve your lifestyle or help you save money.

Remember that not all of these perks will come in the form of *financial* incentives—that doesn't mean they're less valuable.

Once you have gotten acquainted with the types of benefits that are offered by your employer (or a potential employer), you'll be ready to access them. But first...

Read the fine print.

Before you apply for or utilize any benefits, you must first ensure that you understand the terms and conditions of use so that you do not run into trouble. Some benefits—especially those of the savings and insurance varieties—may be regulated. Research the laws and rules that govern workplace benefits in both the industry and the state you work in. Don't forget to research the tax implications of your benefits as well. Some benefits could lower the amount you have to pay in taxes, but others might raise that amount.

Consider enlisting professional help: Benefits consultants and financial advisors are experts at navigating the legal and fiduciary side of things, and they are there to help if you need it. If you are unsure, there is no shame in seeking guidance and advice.

Be mindful of the deadlines.

There may be deadlines and signup periods for certain of your benefits. If you don't make them, you could have to wait a full year before you're allowed to enroll. Check your benefit deadlines, and if you're unsure, ask human resources about registration windows so you don't miss out.

Take advantage of any benefits you can.

To make the most out of your working experience and have a good influence on your financial situation, you should utilize every advantage provided by your company to the utmost extent possible. To this end, take advantage of all the opportunities that are available to you, whether that comes in the form of discounts, savings accounts, company-funded health insurance, or professional development. You have the right to enjoy your employment perks, so make full use of them.

And, as always, review your benefits regularly, and update them as necessary. Your workplace might begin offering new benefits, or you might find that some of the older ones are no longer worth it. Employee perks are just a tool; how you use it is up to you.

Understanding and Negotiating Compensation

No matter how great your benefits may be, though, odds are that your job won't be tenable if your pay is too low. Luckily, the amount of money you make is negotiable.

Negotiation skills are essential if you want to be able to make the kind of money you need to live the kind of life you want. You will be appropriately rewarded for your time and abilities if you know how to negotiate your compensation. By negotiating, you are also giving your employer a chance to see how well you communicate. When you communicate well, you will impress your employer and become known as a person the firm should keep an eye on. As a result, you will advance much more quickly within the organization.

Of course, we cannot overstate the impact that money can have on our lives. Getting paid more to do your job doesn't require much of a sales pitch. However, a sales pitch is essentially what you're going to give to your employer! If you can successfully sell them on the value of your skills and experience, you'll be able to improve your financial stability and security.

But, before you can take that sales pitch to your employer, you first need to have the facts to back it up. You need to understand how your compensation is calculated. Often, it is based on your qualifications, experience, and skills, but sometimes it is determined by market conditions and company guidelines. If you are eligible for bonuses, you may negotiate for higher bonus payments rather than adjusting your underlying salary. You may even negotiate the amount and type of benefits that you receive.

Finally, you will need to research the standard salaries and compensation ranges for similar positions in your industry. Having a point of reference can help make the argument to your employer that your wages should be increased.

Once you have all these items in place, you are ready to have a chat with your employer. The ideal approach to asking for what you want involves extensive planning and research. Prepare your pay negotiation script and approach the conversation with the idea that the other side is a potential negotiating partner.

Keep in mind that you will pay a higher proportion of taxes the more you earn. If your sole emphasis during negotiations is on wanting to earn more money, you will owe more taxes as well. Instead, balance the compensation you want with company benefits. You may significantly lower the amount of money you have to spend on these essentials if you can request benefits like housing allowance, medical assistance, travel allowance, and educational help (Autenrieth, 2022).

Not only will your own life improve as a direct result of a successful negotiation, but the lives of other employees might improve as well. If others see that your efforts in negotiating fair pay are validated, their own sense of worth (both financial and emotional) may go up as a result. They could become motivated to negotiate with upper management, and their own pay could be increased. In essence, you can set a good example.

Remember, employee benefits may not really show up in your bank account as cash, but they still amount to money that your company is prepared to invest in you. Few individuals consider what work perks might be able to achieve for their own finances. You may take advantage of business advantages and have your employer take care of your urgent requirements if you educate yourself sufficiently. You save money as a result, and you may use that money to invest, save, or contribute to your pension. So, when you move from job to job, consider what benefits come with that shift. You don't want to miss extra money in your pocket.

Chapter 9: Retirement Planning

Many people take no care of their money 'til they come nearly to the end of it, and others do just the same with their time. –Johann Wolfgang von Goethe

Financial planning has a running theme of ensuring your stability and satisfaction in the future, and retirement planning is perhaps the best example of that. Getting older is an eventuality that all of us must face. With age often comes degradation—of our health, of our motivation, and even of our finances—but this doesn't have to be the case. If you plan early and plan well, you can ensure that your every need will be taken care of in your retirement. The inexorable march of time is scary enough as it is. Why add financial instability to the mix?

Think of how hard it can be right now to make ends meet financially; now imagine you can no longer work. As you age, your ability (and desire) to work diligently and effectively will wane. You need a strategy, since, as you are aware, you cannot work indefinitely. You don't want to run out of savings, which will mean running out of road: Your smooth and easy retirement will grind to a stop, and you'll be forced to work again. You don't want labor until you drop dead just to fulfill your bare necessities. Thus, it's critical that you start planning for retirement during your career—as soon as possible.

Retirement is an investment you're making in your future well-being. A sound investment plan and diligent long-term saving are required for retirement planning. It takes careful preparation and specialized knowledge to determine how much to save for how long, and which investment vehicles to employ to help you reach your retirement objectives.

There are five phases to retirement planning: deciding when to begin, estimating how much money you'll need, determining priorities, selecting accounts, and selecting investments. The general principle is to invest more vigorously when you're young and then scale down to a more cautious mix of investments as you get closer to retirement (Kagan, 2023b). You may either handle your retirement funds yourself or engage a professional.

This chapter will help you plan for a secure and comfortable retirement by explaining the different types of retirement accounts available to you and offering tips for making the most of your retirement and supplementing your golden years with a little extra income.

The Importance of Retirement Planning

The method of discovering, selecting, and implementing financial solutions that will set you up for a pleasant and secure retirement is known as retirement planning. While making retirement plans, there are a lot of things to think about, including how much money you'll need to meet expenditures, your risk tolerance level, and how much time you still have to be ready.

Planning for retirement should begin long before retirement. The common consensus is that the earlier you begin, the better. The time horizon can make a drastic difference. This may sound like common sense, but it bears repeating: the younger you are, the longer you have to invest, save, and grow your wealth. The earlier you get started, the more time your money will have to multiply, and the more stable your future is likely to be as a result.

Your current age is a key determinant of your retirement-planning process. The steps you'll need to take and the process of planning for retirement will look a lot different for a 45-year-old (who is just beginning to save) than it would for a 25-year-old. In that regard, it's a lot like long-term investment. This is not to say that you're out of luck if you're already 50; it is better to start late than never.

Your magic number—the sum you must have saved to live comfortably in retirement—is extremely individual. However, there are a few generalizations that might help you choose how much to save.

While the quantity you should have in your nest egg is crucial, it's also a good idea to take all of your costs into account. Be sure to factor in the prices of your accommodations, medical coverage, attire, groceries, and travel. You might also want to consider the expenses of entertainment and vacation, as you'll have more spare time. Even if it could be challenging to predict specific numbers, make sure to do so to avoid unpleasant shocks in the future.

Retirement goals are a type of financial goal. While saving for retirement is a financial goal in its own right, it can be subdivided into smaller goals. What kinds of things do you want to achieve during your retirement? How do you want to spend your days? What will it cost you to achieve those goals? Plan for that, budget for that, and ensure you'll have enough cash.

You must also choose the best plan to help you achieve those goals.

Like any other financial strategy, it's important to select the one which best suits your needs and your desired retirement lifestyle. You have to be sure the one you select is worthwhile; you won't have any more money accessible to you once you get older, so you can't afford to make mistakes. You must be confident that your money will be secure and increase significantly. Retirement income changes with time, and you need to have enough money to maintain your standard of living. You should be aware of your retirement possibilities to create a strategy that will work for you in the long run.

Types of Retirement/Pension Accounts

401(k) Plans

The "standard" employee retirement plan is the 401(k). You should remember this type of plan from Chapter 8; if not, here's a quick review.

"A 401(k) is a feature of a qualified profit-sharing plan that allows employees to contribute a portion of their wages to individual accounts" (IRS, n.d.). Many for-profit businesses provide 401(k)s as a perk for their employees. In most cases, you may make a contribution by simply directing a portion of your salary to the retirement plan. A 401(k), like the majority of other retirement plan types, offers tax benefits by lowering your taxable income. Unless you decide to take a payout, the money in your 401(k) grows tax-free. After that, you'll have to pay income tax on the money you take out.

Similar to most other retirement plans, you must be 59 years of age or older to withdraw money without incurring penalties, and you must begin taking withdrawals at age 72. The fact that many businesses match your contributions to 401(k) plans makes them quite appealing. That may be free money. The drawback is that you can only accrue employer contributions over many years (this is known as "vesting"). You will keep all of your payments but may only get a fraction of your company's contributions if you quit the firm before becoming "fully vested".

Pros:

- A simple choice if you work for a company.
- You may receive matching contributions from the employer.

Cons:

- High contribution limits

- Few available investing alternatives

- You will not completely own your employer's matching contributions for several years.

Traditional IRA

These are tax-favored savings accounts that are primarily created and maintained by individuals, as the name (individual retirement arrangement) implies. If you don't have access to a 401(k) plan via your work, a regular IRA may be intriguing because almost anybody with taxable income may contribute to one. Traditional IRAs and 401(k)s are comparable in many ways, including how tax advantages operate. Your contributions lower your taxable income, the investment grows tax-free until you remove it, and both contributions and withdrawals are subject to the same age limits. Your IRA savings are also potentially tax-deductible.

Pros:

- Accessible to everyone
- Offers several investment plan options

Cons:

- Limited contribution amounts.

Roth IRA

A Roth IRA allows for tax-free accumulation and tax-free payouts in retirement. Even high-yield bank accounts can't keep up with the rate of inflation, so your long-term returns will likely be higher if you choose a Roth account. According to Roth IRA regulations, you may withdraw your money whenever you like and won't be required to pay federal taxes as long as you've kept your account for 5 years and are 59 or older. Only money that has previously been taxed can be deposited into a Roth IRA. The main difference between a regular and a Roth IRA is how taxes are treated. Roth IRAs are established with after-tax money, which means that contributions are not tax-exempt, but are tax-free if withdrawals are made during your retirement.

Pros:

- Overall, you could pay less tax.
- Retirement funds are withdrawable tax-free.
- Contribution and withdrawal have age restrictions.

Cons

- No contribution tax break
- Subject to income limitations
- Limited contribution amounts

Non-Qualified Deferred Compensation Plans

This is a type of retirement arrangement that enables a select group of highly compensated employees to benefit from tax advantages by deferring a higher proportion of their pay (and current income taxes) than is permitted under an IRS-approved qualified retirement arrangement. You need to be a high earner to qualify for this type of retirement plan because it only works if you can make large contributions every month.

Pros:

- No annual contribution cap is imposed by the IRS on the amount that you may put into your 401(k). An NQDC scheme has no upper limit.

- Tax benefits: You will have less taxable income after making your deferral option, which may decrease your tax bracket.

Cons:

● Money withdrawals are only permitted from nonqualified deferred compensation plans on specific dates. As with a 401(k) or other eligible retirement plans, you cannot make an early withdrawal

● The Employee Retirement Income Security Act does not provide any protection for your money (ERISA).

Tax benefits are offered by all retirement plans as a motivator to save for retirement. Many retirement plan types have different restrictions regarding withdrawals, contribution caps, and when you must pay income taxes. There are plans made for employees, self-employed people, businesspersons, and for everyone else. Due to the numerous factors in these plans, any person may or may not be qualified for their tax benefits, therefore it's crucial to speak with a qualified tax expert about your unique situation (Appleby, 2022).

Options For Retirement Income

While you may have saved enough to meet your requirements, there are instances when your retirement savings and pension plans may just not be enough. You should have fallback options in case your savings are insufficient by the time you retire due to the changing nature of the economy.

Social Security

Although the majority of retirees are eligible for social security payments, these are frequently insufficient. Furthermore, social security retirement payments are primarily designed for those with lower incomes, and are only available to those who retired with an annual income of less than $100,000. Just around 40% of your pre-retirement earnings will be replaced by Social Security retirement payments (Hughes, 2020). Social security should by no means be discounted, but living on these payments alone will scarcely cover your bare necessities.

As a result, it is imperative to develop long-term alternate sources of income.

Income Annuities

This is an agreement between you and an insurance company where you pay a lump sum and receive that sum over time as periodic payments. You may use annuities to create a guaranteed income stream for the rest of your life, or for a specific amount of time.

The money might potentially grow tax-deferred while it is with the insurance company. As you begin receiving payments, you might decide on a steady income source or adjust your expenses to keep up with inflation. You may also decide whether this income will be paid throughout the course of only your life, or the lives of you and another person.

A percentage of your retirement assets may benefit from annuities, which may offer security, long-term growth, and income. Annuities are a common tool used by retirees to supplement their assured sources of income and cover their ongoing needs.

Long-Term Care Insurance

If you have long-term care insurance, you might find yourself drawing upon that insurance money during retirement, when you're more likely than ever to need long-term care. This can be another way to supplement your income and cover your medical bills.

Return on Investment

Your investments can continue to pay out returns during your retirement. This is another reason why long-term investing is a fantastic idea. The income from your investment portfolio is provided through a total return strategy in the form of interest, dividend income, and capital gains. This kind of portfolio makes investments in a well-balanced and varied selection of bond and equity funds.

To address the demands of those planning for retirement that might last 20 to 30 years or longer, this is one strategy to establish a retirement portfolio. You should review and adjust your portfolio regularly to ensure that it supports your retirement goals.

Leasing

If you have acquired real estate property while investing, you can sell it for a profit, but you can also rent it out as a source of passive income. There is no need to lease the entire property; by renting out additional space in your home or garage that might be used as living quarters. Even though the amount you may earn often depends on your location and the quantity of living space you give, it's typically a sure source of revenue that doesn't require you to put in much time or effort. On specialized websites, you may locate individuals who could be interested in renting out a portion of your residence.

In a similar vein, you may be able to cut costs by downsizing and moving to a smaller home or more affordable area.

Home Equity

Taking out home equity loans or HELOCs can allow retirees to effectively access cash from their home equity.

Reverse mortgages involve using your home as collateral, but unlike a regular mortgage, you are not required to pay down the loan for as long as you live in your home. This comes with the downside of decreasing your overall home equity—a reverse mortgage could present problems if you ever want to sell, but you will have access to funds in the meantime. This can be a way to stay financially stable during retirement.

Part-Time or Freelance Work

If you're the more actionable sort, you can also seek out a part-time job that's within your ability level during retirement. You may use your gained skills, experience, and knowledge to work as a freelancer if you are an expert in a certain sector. The majority of freelancing jobs offer a great deal of flexibility, letting retirees choose their working hours while still having time for other commitments. Also, a lot of freelance jobs are remote, so you hardly ever need to visit the place of employment.

Retirement-age individuals and anyone with free time might increase their income by caring for local pets, for example. A pet sitter is frequently hired by pet owners who don't have the time to walk, wash, feed, or spend time with their animals. Taking care of neighborhood dogs might be a potential source of income if you have a passion for animals and some expertise in pet ownership.

Tips and Strategies for Maximizing Retirement Contributions and Benefits

Planning for retirement is crucial because it provides life security. By making retirement plans, you provide yourself the ability to do what you like when you're older and not have to worry about your financial situation. Instead, you can keep living your normal life. In addition to providing an additional source of income, retirement planning paves the way for achieving life goals, managing medical crises, and being financially independent. Here are some additional tips:

Maximize your contributions.

By contributing the greatest possible sum at one time, you are making an investment in your own future. If making large contributions is not feasible given your current life situation, you can always start with more moderate contributions and then increase them gradually over time. It is also a good idea to put your raises and bonuses into your retirement account.

Don't forget employee benefits.

If your employer offers matching contributions, take full advantage by making the maximum contribution. This can effectively double your retirement savings.

If a health savings account is covered as part of your employee benefits package, take advantage of that as well.

Consolidate retirement accounts.

Much like debt consolidation, consolidating multiple retirement accounts has the potential to lower fees and streamline your retirement planning process. Having fewer accounts to manage can reduce stress.

If you have a traditional IRA, you may also explore conversion options to change it to a Roth IRA, as the latter are widely considered more beneficial. In particular, you should get a hidden Roth IRA because it can help you save more money in addition to your retirement savings.

Keep taxes in mind.

There are tax credits for retirement savings; there may be advantages to claiming two plan contributions rather than consolidating. And don't forget the tax-deferring benefits that retirement accounts offer!

Chapter 10: Technology and Tools in Financial Planning

Now that we are in the digital age, anything and everything can be enhanced using just a few keystrokes on your smartphone, laptop, or computer. Finances are no exception. Plenty of tools and technologies exist to help you streamline and automate every step of your financial journey, from simple expense tracking and bill payment to complex investment strategies. It's no longer necessary to physically visit a bank or a stock broker; instead, you can invest and trade entirely online using applications or websites. This final chapter will cover everything you need to know to become more digitally savvy, and minimize risk while doing so.

The Benefits of Financial Technology

When it comes to your finances, you can make better judgments if you use technology. As a citizen of the modern world, you are better-equipped than previous generations to make informed financial decisions, because technology and tools are not there only to provide convenience. They can also

- offer personalized insights into your own finances.

- allow you to monitor your finances from anywhere.

- help you stay informed of risks and opportunities.

- provide access to updated financial information in real-time, whether it's your own account or the global stock market.

- improve your time management.

● facilitate easy communication with licensed financial experts and advisors who can give you individualized guidance based on your objectives.

● make it easier to understand and organize financial documents.

● assist in the processes of financial management, budgeting, and investment.

The nicest part of it all is that everything can be simplified, everything will function without a hitch, and you can concentrate on the rest of your life.

Personal Finance Apps and Online Tools

There are thousands of apps out there in the market, and you can't test them all out—so we've broken them down by category to help you know where to start. There is broad overlap between many of these apps, and that's not a bad thing; it offers you more freedom to find one that suits you best.

Aggregation apps such as Yodlee and Plaid receive financial data from banks and customers around the world, and use it to give individuals a form of personalized, data-driven wealth management, whereby people can monitor and analyze their finances in depth. These apps can essentially eliminate the need for bank statements, as you can have an e-statement ready at any time.

Personal finance aggregation is the force behind many financial apps. This crucial capability allows users to view all of their accounts in one place.

Budgeting apps make it simpler to keep track of your costs by providing you with a single, comprehensive view of your finances. These apps use data aggregation to seamlessly import your transactions from all of your bank accounts into one location, and then integrate those transactions into your budget. Often, budgeting apps provide graphics and trackers that can help you visualize your finances. Many offer additional features: Some apps, like Intuit Mint, give you the built-in ability to negotiate your bills with providers, while others, like EveryDollar, allow you to communicate with personal finance specialists who can assist you with your budgeting goals. These are also notable for their ability to streamline emergency fund planning and contributions.

Investment management apps offer an interface through which you can make new investments. They too provide you with a convenient place to view and track your various investments. Most will allow you to purchase custom-built portfolios which are already diversified. Each app provides its own incentives. Robinhood allows you to purchase stocks and ETFs without any commission fees; Acorns will round up your investments to the nearest dollar. Both of these apps give you retirement accounts, so you have somewhere to put your investment. Robinhood even matches 1% of your retirement contributions.

Financial management software can help you with all of the above: monitoring your finances, budgeting, investing, and saving for retirement. Empower (formerly known as Personal Capital), Quicken, and Vanguard are some more apps that will cover your financial bases.

Credit management apps offer you an easy way to check your credit score and monitor your credit at a glance—no credit card required. They will provide credit reports, along with personalized insights on your credit and tips for improving it. They also help you track any changes. Credit Sesame and Credit Karma are two free apps of this type. Mint also offers free credit reports and credit monitoring.

Tax preparation and filing apps aggregate the IRS rules and schedules for the current tax year, which will save you time. These apps aim to streamline the filing process so that you can easily determine which deductions you qualify for, maximize your returns, and minimize your costs. Essentially, they perform the process of tax planning for you. Using apps could result in a more profitable tax return than filing on your own.

On the IRS's website, you can find a list of government-approved third-party software providers with whom you can file for free (unless state fees apply). Some of these include FreeTaxUSA, TaxAct, and 1040NOW.NET, although the list is updated yearly (along with the tax regulations and deadlines). TurboTax and H&R Block are some popular non-IRS-affiliated tax apps.

Bill payment apps let you monitor, manage, and schedule payments. Like most financial apps, they aggregate all of your invoices and bank accounts in a single app, precluding the need to juggle different accounts. Prism is one such app. The software automatically keeps track of your invoices and notifies you when they are due. It also enables you to schedule payments in advance.

Digital wallets and payment processors, such as Venmo, PayPal, CashApp, ApplePay, and Square, enable you to transfer or receive money instantly, rather than waiting days for a bank account transfer to go through. They offer a place to store money temporarily, and the option to transfer it to your bank if you wish. These are accepted forms of payment at some stores, but are mainly used for online transactions and person-to-person transfers. There are also digital wallets specifically for storing and sending cryptocurrency, such as Coinbase, Binance, and Trust Wallet.

This list of financial apps is not exhaustive. You are free to explore and find your own; however, you will need to ensure that you remain safe while doing so.

Selecting and Safely Using Financial Technology

Read up on the features and capabilities. Once you understand the specifics of what each app or site can do for you, you'll be able to select the one that best fits your needs.

Whatever program you choose, you must ensure that you know how to use it correctly and effectively. And a major part of that is security—not just as in "financial security," but as in "data security."

Reputable financial apps will clearly state their security measures on their website's home page or store download page. Data encryption is a must when you're dealing with credit card numbers and other confidential financial data. Some apps provide fraud detection. Before downloading or using a financial app of any sort, read all the fine print. It is absolutely crucial to know what is being done with your data, and what measures are in place to protect it.

It's generally safer to download software from trusted vendors, such as the Apple iStore and Google Play Store. These marketplaces inspect and verify the apps that they host, which adds an increased degree of security (although there is still a chance that malware could slip through undetected). This is why it's important to read the app reviews before downloading it, as an added measure of safety. A good app should have at least four stars. Once you are assured of an app's trustworthiness, you can download it.

Consider trying out apps to improve each area of your financial management: budgeting and expense tracking, investment monitoring and management, financial document handling, and communication with financial advisors. This can help you stay informed and on top of your decisions.

Once you've selected an app, review the user interface to see if it's simple to use. Like budgets and other financial tools, apps should be a help rather than a hindrance.

You should also keep your technology and tools updated and maintained to ensure that they continue to perform at their best. Check frequently for updates, which could enhance security measures or speed up the operation of the tool in question.

Data Security and Privacy Protection

As you know, it is important to monitor your accounts and transactions regularly. Apps can help you do so, and alert you of suspicious activity or fraud as soon as it happens. But remember that even trustworthy applications may be targeted by hackers, scammers, and cybercriminals—though, of course, the same is true of brick-and-mortar financial institutions. The key is to be careful with how you handle your data, and not give criminals (cyber or otherwise) any opportunities to take advantage of you.

Every time you use a computer or mobile device to access the internet, you leave a digital trail. This is especially true if you use financial software. Together with your name, bank information, email address, and phone number, every financial app keeps track of what happens to your money, where you spend it, and where it comes from. This information can be used by hackers to target and damage you. It's critical to take precautions when engaging online.

Every financial app has security precautions in place that you should be aware of, and you should also be aware of your legal rights if you are exposed when utilizing one of the tools (Tech, 2020). Most reputable financial apps are encrypted for your safety, but that doesn't mean you shouldn't also take every other precaution available to you. The importance of data security and privacy cannot be understated. This is your hard-earned money we're talking about, after all.

Even if it seems inconvenient, it is worth it to use strong passwords with a mix of letters, numbers, and symbols, and to opt into security measures like two-factor authentication and fraud alerts. Encrypt your data when you have the option.

You must exercise great vigilance and take action to obtain powerful antivirus software to protect your devices and networks, as certain viruses will steal data. Think of it as another form of insurance and risk management. Anti-malware programs are well worth the money, since they protect the rest of your money.

Whether you're using a web browser, don't enter any financial info unless you are absolutely certain it is secure to do so. Look for a lock icon on the top of your browser, next to the URL. This indicates a secure connection, and minimizes the chances of third parties stealing any data you might input.

Be cautious of phishing scams, where criminals will often pose as your financial institution and attempt to acquire your financial information. Even your bank should not ask for your account password or your credit card number. Always ask the other party to verify their identity. If there is any doubt, make that transaction in person. Never open suspicious emails or click on links that promise prizes. Anything that appears genuine but sounds too wonderful to be true is most likely a scam. Free and quick money does not exist; scammers are cunning and will take advantage of your desperation.

Finally, in the case of tax-filing apps, you should ensure that any program you select is approved by the IRS or federal government.

Financial digital apps can simplify and streamline your money management process and accelerate your financial growth, but you must be careful to ensure that your data is protected: if you don't safeguard yourself, you could lose everything you've worked so hard to achieve.

Conclusion

It's not how much money you make, but how much money you keep, how hard it works for you, and how many generations you keep it for. –Robert Kiyosaki

Personal finance is more than just money: it is your legacy. If you know how to use money well, and let it work for you instead of you working for it, you will leave something behind for future generations. If you've realized you've been making bad financial decisions, don't fret: You know better now. If you start investing time and effort (and, of course, money), there is still ample time to improve your finances and your life.

Making changes might be overwhelming, but you've got this. Start by doing one thing; evaluate the results, and once you're satisfied, move on to the next thing. Eventually, you'll discover that you are completely financially savvy, have a strong financial portfolio, and can optimize everything you do using digital financial tools.

This book was created to level the playing field, provide you with a springboard to manage your money more effectively, and attain a better financial position, now and in the future. You have the power to create a comfortable existence and a decent standard of living. Money is life, and this book has made that point repeatedly: The better you are at managing your money, the better your life will be.

You've now realized that having a clear understanding of where you are now and where you want to be in terms of finances is essential. Where you are right now, how much money you make, what benefits you receive, and how much debt you have all come into play. Understanding all of this will enable you to create specific financial objectives for the person you want to become—someone with a retirement plan and a sound investing strategy.

This book has taught you how to properly manage debt, negotiate a higher salary, make the most of your employee benefits, and plan for the future without straining yourself in the present. For all of these, you must manage your money wisely.

The main goal of personal finance is to ensure that you can meet all of your financial demands. Money is required to generate more money, and this should be your ultimate objective. You can only achieve true financial independence when you have a lot of money.

To this end, you may occasionally need to practice frugal living, since life is full of expenditures. You need self-control to not squander money and only use it for what is required. Owning a home, paying for maintenance and upkeep, maintaining a car, receiving quality medical treatment, and purchasing nutritious food all come at a price. Any of these costs may burn a hole in your wallet, and will only increase over time due to inflation and other economic factors.

It's advantageous to have income, but how much do you keep? As you go through your life, you need to save money for investments, retirement, and emergency funds. You can hold onto your money by budgeting and keeping your expenses in check. You need to be aware of how you are spending, but if you can create and follow a budgeting strategy, you won't be spending continuously.

Your ability to allocate funds where they are required, invest, save, and spend responsibly will determine how things turn out. You will never have to worry about retirement if you are good at money management. If you are smart about your investments and savings, you should have enough passive income streams built up over the years to support your retirement. You'll thank yourself later.

You might not be able to accomplish everything in this book right away, but you've been given the tools to start. Realistically, it will take 10 to 20 years to establish a solid financial position. For certain people, depending on their income and circumstances, it may take less time, but in a perfect world it will still take longer than 10 years to see the results of your labor. Start saving for retirement if you can't at least create an emergency fund or savings account. If you are unable to invest, utilize debt (responsibly, of course) to purchase necessities like a house or automobile. You may pay off your debt considerably faster if you follow the strategies you've been given.

Remember that Rome wasn't built in a day, and carefully weigh all of your alternatives before selecting the one that will take you forward. With time and practice, you'll develop a strong sense of independence and self-reliance.

Best of luck in your financial journey.

End Note

Please don't be hesitant to give a review if you enjoyed reading this book and found it valuable. If you've learned something new, let others know! Everyone should be successful, in excellent financial standing, and able to live comfortably. This book only seeks to fill a societal vacuum caused by inadequate financial education. You may use it as a go-to resource to improve your financial management skills. And, if possible, please share with us what you've learned or implemented, and how your finances have changed as a result of this book. It would inspire others to follow suit, and the mission would have been completed.

My deepest regards to every reader.

Georgiana Golden

Glossary

Annual Percentage Rates (APR): A figure that expresses the entire cost of getting a loan as a proportion of the loan's principal. The APR on a credit card or loan seeks to provide an accurate representation of how much borrowing money will cost.

Annuity: An insurance policy that banking institutions have created and disseminated with the goal of returning invested money as a fixed additional income in the future. Annuities are bought or invested in by investors using lump-sum contributions or monthly premiums.

Bankruptcy: A legal procedure through which individuals or other businesses that owe money to lenders but are unable to pay them back may request remission from some or all of their obligations. Bankruptcy is often enforced by a court order that is frequently requested by the debtor.

Bonds: A form of debt security. Bonds are issued by creditors to attract capital from investors ready to extend a loan to them for a specific period of time. When you purchase a bond, you are making a loan to the issuer, which might be a corporation, state, or municipality.

Capital Gains: The profit made by selling an item that has appreciated in value while being held.

Certificate of Deposit (CD): An account that keeps a certain sum of money for a specific length of time.

Credit: The agreement that permits one party to give money or resources to another, with the understanding that the second party will not instantaneously compensate the first party, but will instead repay or return the funds at a later time.

Creditor: A person or business that owes money to another.

Credit Card: A line of credit where users are given a payment card that enables them to pay for goods and services depending on the cardholder's accumulated debt.

Credit Counseling: A service that offers advice on budgeting, financial planning, personal finance, and consumer lending.

Credit Management: The process of approving credit, establishing the conditions under which it is issued, collecting this payment when it is outstanding, and maintaining compliance with the company's credit policy, among other credit-related tasks.

Credit Portfolio: A group of credit risks that are accumulated as a result of financial intermediation activity.

Credit Score: A numerical representation of your payment history and credit history which offers a perspective on how to handle your debt.

Commodity: A fundamental item that is used in trade and may be swapped out for other items of the same kind. The most frequent use of commodities is as raw materials for the creation of other products or services.

Data Security: The method of safeguarding data throughout its lifetime from illegal access and data corruption. Data protection techniques such as encryption software, authentication, and key management safeguard data across all platforms and applications.

Debit Card: A physical card that enables its owner to make purchases by electronically transferring money from their bank account.

Debt: Money owed to a lender.

Debtor: A person or business that owes money. The debtor is known as a **borrower** if the obligation takes the form of a loan from a financial institution.

Debt Consolidation: The procedure of taking out a new loan to pay off existing debts and liabilities. A single payment is made in order to pay off several debts.

Debt Management: A strategy where budgeting and financial planning are employed with the objective of reducing your present debt and working toward its elimination.

Derivatives: Financial agreements made between two or more parties that draw (or derive) their worth from a base asset, base group of assets, or base reference point. A derivative may be traded over-the-counter or on a marketplace.

Dividend-Bearing Account: A sub-account used to receive and keep cash dividends paid by the plan sponsor on workplace securities.

Employee Assistance Program (EAP): A program that provides employees with a variety of different benefits.

Exchange-Traded Funds (ETFs): Investments that trade on exchanges and often follow a certain index. You may purchase and sell a variety of assets during market hours when you invest in an ETF, possibly reducing your risk and exposure.

Federal Insurance Contributions Act: A federal payroll deduction made by both employers and employees to pay for Social Security and Medicare, two government programs that offer benefits for retirees, people with disabilities or impairments, and the children of workers who have died.

FICO Model: A framework used to measure creditworthiness.

Financial Goals: Targets set by an individual to achieve financial milestones or plans.

Financial Literacy: The capacity to comprehend and utilize different financial abilities, such as investing, budgeting, and personal financial management, successfully.

Financial Planning: The creation of a document based on careful analysis of your income and expenses, with the intention of helping you become more aware of your financial situation at all times. It sets significant short- and long-term financial objectives.

Financial Portfolio: A group of financial assets such as closed-end funds, exchange-traded funds, equities, securities, consumables, currency, and cash equivalents.

Financially Savvy: Describes a person who is knowledgeable in handling expenses, credit, and other financial concerns.

Healthcare Spending Account: An account that you fund with money and use to cover certain out-of-pocket medical expenses. On this cash, you don't pay taxes. This indicates that the money you placed away will save you money equivalent to the taxes you would have had to pay.

High-Yield Account: A kind of savings account that often yields 20 to 25 times the average national yield on a conventional savings account.

Individual Retirement Account (IRA): A long-term savings account used by an individual with the goal of saving for retirement.

Insurance: A form of protection against financial loss whereby, in return for a fee, one party commits to make up for another party's losses, damages, or accidents.

Insurance Coverage: The degree to which a person or entity's risk and responsibility are covered by insurance services.

Interest-Bearing Account: A sort of bank account that offers interest to the consumer in exchange for their money being deposited at the bank. Depending on the terms and limitations of the account, each bank will give a different return and interest rate.

Interest Rate: The percentage amount that the lender charges the borrower in addition to the principal amount.

Internal Revenue Service (IRS): The United States Federal Government's revenue service, in charge of managing the Internal Revenue Code and gathering U.S. federal taxes.

Legal Loophole: A vulnerability that enables a person or company to evade the application of a law or limitation without actually breaking the law

Leverage: Any strategy that involves borrowing money to make purchases in the hopes that future earnings will be much greater than the cost of borrowing.

Loan: An agreement whereby one or more people, businesses, or other entities lend money to other people, businesses, or entities.

Long-term Investor: An investor that has the financial wherewithal to be patient for a prolonged period of time, and is prepared to assume some risk in the hope of earning benefits that may be larger.

Money Market Account: A form of deposit account where account holders receive interest on the money they deposit.

Mutual Fund: A professionally-managed investment fund that combines the funds of several participants to buy assets.

Payment Default(s): One or more missed payments to lenders.

Policy Holder: A person or organization that has an insurance policy in their name.

Portfolio Diversification: The act of broadening your investments to limit your vulnerability to any one asset class. This routine is intended to gradually lessen the volatility of your portfolio.

Reverse Budgeting: A "pay yourself first" budget that prioritizes savings over payments on debt and other expenses.

Risk Management: The procedure for locating, evaluating, and managing risks to an investment's capital and profits that arise from legal, tactical, financial, and security issues.

Roth Retirement Account (IRA): Is a retirement account that you may fund with after-tax money. Your payments and profits can grow tax-free, and you can withdraw them tax- and penalty-free until age 59, even though there are no advantages for the current tax year.

Social Security: A federal-government-run initiative which uses taxes deposited into a trust fund to provide assistance for the elderly and disabled.

Stocks: A type of investment that symbolizes corporate ownership by purchasing shares.

Stock Market: A platform of securities exchange where buyers and sellers of publicly-listed company shares transact business. A procedure known as an initial public offering allows private firms to list shares of their stock on a market.

Tax: A levy that is placed on a citizen by a government agency; must be paid in order to cover government expenses and other public expenditures.

Tax Credit: A condition that lowers a taxpayer's overall tax obligation, dollar-for-dollar.

Tax-Efficient: Refers to a strategy that reduces your tax burden.

Tax Losses: A situation where total costs exceed total receipts (under the tax reporting regulations of the relevant government jurisdiction).

Tax Planning: The examination of a financial position or strategy to see how well each component cooperates to enable an individual to pay the least amount of taxes.

Tax Preparation: The process of producing tax returns, often income tax returns, frequently for someone other than the taxpayer, and typically for payment.

Tax Regulations: All Tax-related laws, regulations, and other official pronouncements in nations where the company is subject to taxation, as well as any international treaties (including guidelines, restrictions, and other relevant agreements in the respective country) and any other legally enforceable authority that applies in a taxing jurisdiction.

Tax Savings: A decrease in the taxes that an individual, corporation, or other taxpayers have to pay. As a result, after submitting an income tax return, the amount of income tax withheld or the overall tax burden may be reduced.

Vesting: The process of gradually acquiring an asset, such as stock options or employer-matched 401(k) contributions.

Zero-Based Budget: A system of budgeting that demands justification and approval of all spending for each new budgetary period.

References

Anspach, D. (2021, December 18). *Emergency Cash Reserves: How Much Money You Should Have Set Aside*. The Balance. https://www.thebalancemoney.com/how-much-should-i-have-in-my-emergency-fund-2388353

Appleby, D. (2022, December 21). *The Best Retirement Plans to Build Your Nest Egg*. Investopedia. https://www.investopedia.com/articles/retirement/08/best-plan.asp

Autenrieth, N. (2022, May 18). *Guide to negotiating the Best Compensation Package*. TopResume. https://www.topresume.com/career-advice/guide-to-negotiating-the-best-overall-compensation-package

Bareham, H. (2023, Feb 1). *How to pay off Credit Card Debt*. Bankrate. https://www.bankrate.com/finance/credit-cards/ways-to-pay-off-credit-card-debt/

Beers, B. (2022, August 8). *10 ETF Concerns That Investors Shouldn't Overlook*. Investopedia. https://www.investopedia.com/articles/mutualfund/07/etf_downside.asp

Bringle, L. (2021, October 8). *The 3 Main Types of Credit Explained. Self.* https://www.self.inc/blog/types-of-credit

Capital One. (2021, July 28). *Types of debt: Understanding different debts*. Capital One. https://www.capitalone.com/learn-grow/money-management/types-of-debt/

Chen, J. (2023, March 31). Private Equity Explained With Examples and Ways to Invest. Investopedia. https://www.investopedia.com/terms/p/privateequity.asp

Consumer Financial Protection Bureau. (2021, June 23). *What is a co-signer?.* CFPB. https://www.consumerfinance.gov/ask-cfpb/what-is-a-co-signer-en-745/#:~:text=A%20co%2Dsigner%20takes%20full,the%20borrow [1].

Crail, C. (2022, Aug 18). *Does Your State Require You to Have Health Insurance? Forbes.* https://www.forbes.com/advisor/health-insurance/do-you-have-to-have-health-insurance/

Discover. (2023, February 22). *Where should you keep your emergency fund?* Discover Bank, Member FDIC. https://www.discover.com/online-banking/banking-topics/where-to-keep-emergency-fund/

Egan, J. (2022, September 8). *The main types of debt and how to handle each.* Forbes. https://www.forbes.com/advisor/debt-relief/types-of-debt/

---

1. https://www.consumerfinance.gov/ask-cfpb/what-is-a-co-signer-en-745/#_853ae90f0351324bd73ea615e6487517__4c761f170e016836ff84498202b99827__853ae90f0351324bd73ea615e6487517_text_43ec3e5dee6e706af7766fffea512721_A_0bcef9c45bd8a48eda1b26eb0c61c869_20co_0bcef9c45bd8a48eda1b26eb0c61c869_2Dsigner_0bcef9c45bd8a48eda1b26eb0c61c869_20takes_0bcef9c45bd8a48eda1b26eb0c61c869_20full_c0cb5f0fcf239ab3d9c1fcd31fff1efc_the_0bcef9c45bd8a48eda1b26eb0c61c869_20borrower_0bcef9c45bd8a48eda1b26eb0c61c869_20doesn_3590cb8af0bbb9e78c343b52b93773c9_t_0bcef9c45bd8a48eda1b26eb0c61c869_20pay

Employee benefits: The Importance of Employee Benefits. Virgin Pulse. (2022, February 27). https://www.virginpulse.com/learning/employee-benefits/

Fernando, J. (2023, March 31). *Derivatives: Types, Considerations, and Pros and Cons.* Investopedia. https://www.investopedia.com/terms/d/derivative.asp

The 5 Key Benefits of Debt Consolidation You Need to Know. Eloan. (n.d.). https://www.eloan.com/blog/personal-finance/5-key-benefits-debt-consolidation

Fontinelle, A. (2022, October 12). *How to set financial goals for your future.* Investopedia. https://www.investopedia.com/articles/personal-finance/100516/setting-financial-goals/

Fowler, J. (2022, August 12). *Why an emergency fund is more important than ever.* Investopedia. https://www.investopedia.com/financial-edge/0812/why-an-emergency-fund-is-important.aspx

Gillespie, L. (2022, December 20.). *Credit scores in 2022: Statistics and how to build your credit.* Bankrate. https://www.bankrate.com/personal-finance/credit/how-to-improve-your-credit-score/

Glassdoor Team. (2016, January 12). Glassdoor. glassdoor.com/blog/glassdoors-5-job-trends-watch-2016/

Grossman, A. (2022, April 2). *7 S.M.A.R.T. Financial Goals Worksheets (All Free!).* Frugal Confessions. https://www.frugalconfessions.com/money-goals/smart-financial-goals-worksheets/

Grossman, A. L. (2021, October 9). *5 essential types of financial goals (plus 24 financial goal examples)*. Frugal Confessions. https://www.frugalconfessions.com/money-goals/types-of-financial-goals/

Haughey, D. (2014, December 13). *A Brief History of SMART Goals*. Project Smart. https://www.projectsmart.co.uk/smart-goals/brief-history-of-smart-goals.php

Holton, L. J. (2021, August 13). *The Benefits of Using Technology to Help Manage Your Money*. iGrad. https://www.igrad.com/articles/the-benefits-of-using-technology-to-help-manage-your-money

How to effectively manage & pay off credit card debt. InCharge Debt Solutions. (2021, December 13). https://www.incharge.org/understanding-debt/credit-card/how-to-manage-credit-card-debt/

Hubbard, Z. (2020, July 9). Struggling to Stick to a Budget? Try a Values-Based Budget Instead. Greenspring Advisors. https://greenspringadvisors.com/insight/struggling-to-stick-to-a-budget-try-a-values-based-budget-instead/

Huddleston, C. (2023, February 3). *Best tips on how to Get Life Insurance for the first time*. Forbes. https://www.forbes.com/advisor/life-insurance/best-tips-first-time-buyers/

Hughes, R. A. (2020, October 26). *Why retirement planning is important*. Bull Oak Capital. https://bulloakcapital.com/blog/why-retirement-planning-is-important/

The importance of a long-term outlook when investing. Shepherds Friendly. (2022, May 20). https://www.shepherdsfriendly.co.uk/resources/importance-long-term-outlook-investing/

Investopedia. (2022, July 13). *How to Build an Emergency Fund.* https://www.investopedia.com/personal-finance/how-to-build-emergency-fund/

Investopedia. (2022, October 3). *Commodities.* https://www.investopedia.com/ask/answers/022315/what-are-tradable-commodities.asp

IRS. (2022). *Publication 463 (2022), Travel, Gift, and Car Expenses.* irs.gov/publications/p463#en_US_2022_publink10009980

IRS. (2023, January 11). *Credits and Deductions for Individuals.* Internal Revenue Service. https://www.irs.gov/credits-deductions-for-individuals

IRS. (n.d.). *Types of Retirement Plans.* https://www.irs.gov/retirement-plans/plan-sponsor/types-of-retirement-plans

Jones, K. (2017, February 15). *The Most Desirable Employee Benefits.* Harvard Business Review. https://hbr.org/2017/02/the-most-desirable-employee-benefits

Kagan, J. (2023a, February 21). *Tax planning: What it is, how it works, examples.* Investopedia. https://www.investopedia.com/terms/t/tax-planning.asp

Kagan, J. (2023b, January 25). *5 Retirement Planning Steps to Take.* Investopedia. https://www.investopedia.com/articles/retirement/11/5-steps-to-retirement-plan.asp

Kagan, J. (2023c, March 31). *Insurance: Definition, How It Works, and Main Types of Policies.* Investopedia. https://www.investopedia.com/terms/i/insurance.asp

Kenton, W. (2021, March 1). *What Is Risk Management in Finance, and Why Is It Important?* Investopedia. https://www.investopedia.com/terms/r/riskmanagement.asp

Kilroy, A. (2022, May 24). *8 Different Types Of Insurance Policies And Coverage You Need.* Forbes. https://www.forbes.com/advisor/insurance/types-of-insurance-policies/

Kopp, C. M. (2022, July 4). *How Tax-Loss Harvesting Works for Average Investors.* Investopedia. https://www.investopedia.com/articles/taxes/08/tax-loss-harvesting.asp

Kurt, D. (2022, February 9). *Emergency Fund.* Investopedia. https://www.investopedia.com/terms/e/emergency_fund.asp

Majaski, A. (2022, June 11). *Mortgages vs. Home Equity Loans: What's the Difference?.* Investopedia. https://www.investopedia.com/mortgage/heloc/differences/

Mint. (2020, Dec 11). *Survey: 65% of Americans Have No Idea How Much They Spent Last Month.* Intuit Mint.

https://mint.intuit.com/blog/budgeting/spending-knowledge-survey/

Moore, A. (2014, May 14). *5 awesome and totally free money management tools.* XY Planning Network. https://blog.xyplanningnetwork.com/consumer-blog/5free-money-management-tools

Phil. (2022, September 23). *15 Types of Investments: What Will Make You the Most Money?.* Rule #1 Investing. https://wp.ruleoneinvesting.com/investing-guide/types-of-investments/

Probasco, J. (2023, March 28). *Money Market Account: How It Works and How It Differs From Other Bank Accounts.* Investopedia. https://www.investopedia.com/terms/m/moneymarketaccount.asp

Schmoll, J. (2018, March 6). *3 benefits of using a tax professional.* Frugal Rules. https://www.frugalrules.com/using-tax-professional/

Siroto, J. (2023, March 8). *7 Different Types of Budgeting Methods.* SoFi. https://www.sofi.com/learn/content/types-of-budgeting-methods/

Talerico, A. (2023, March 4). *SMART Goals.* CFI, Corporate Finance Institute. https://corporatefinanceinstitute.com/resources/management/smart-goal/

Team Acko. (2022, December 12). *Types of Insurance.* Acko General Insurance. https://www.acko.com/articles/general-info/types-of-insurance/

Tech, I. S. G. (2020, December 28). *The role of firewalls in defending your data.* ISG Technology. https://www.isgtech.com/the-role-of-firewalls-in-defending-your-data/

10 reasons risk management matters for all employees. (n.d.). Risk Management Software. https://www.clearrisk.com/risk-management-blog/risk-management-matters-for-all-employees-0-0-0-0

Top 10 benefits of working with a professional tax relief firm. (n.d.). Optima Tax Relief. https://optimataxrelief.com/benefits-professional-tax-relief-firm/

Traulsen, C. J. (n.d.). *The importance of investing for the long term.* Morningstar UK. https://www.morningstar.co.uk/uk/news/59663/the-importance-of-investing-for-the-long-term.aspx

Tucci, L. (2023, January 17). *What is risk management and why is it important?* Security. https://www.techtarget.com/searchsecurity/definition/What-is-risk-management-and-why-is-it-important

12 Best Personal Finance Software for Windows 10 and Mac. (2023, February 9). Software Testing Help. https://www.softwaretestinghelp.com/personal-finance-software/

US Securities and Exchange Commission. (n.d.) *What are bonds?* Investor.gov. https://www.investor.gov/introduction-investing/investing-basics/investment-products/bonds-or-fixed-income-products/bonds#:~:text=A%20bond%20is%20a%20debt,government%2C%

What is budgeting and why is it important? My Money Coach. (n.d.). https://www.mymoneycoach.ca/budgeting/what-is-a-budget-planning-forecasting

What is credit and why is it important: A beginner's guide to credit. PNC Insights. (n.d.). https://www.pnc.com/insights/personal-finance/spend/what-is-credit-and-why-is-it-important.html

Why are employee benefits important? types and advantages. (n.d.). https://www.indeed.com/career-advice/career-development/why-are-employee-benefits-important

Why retirement planning is more important than you think. Lifehack. (2016, December 31). https://www.lifehack.org/512533/why-retirement-planning-more-important-than-you-think